HEAVEN
AND
HELL

Books by Peter Toon

Development of Doctrine in the Church
Evangelical Theology 1833-1856
God's Statesman: The Life of Dr. John Owen
Justification and Sanctification
The Anglican Way: Evangelical and Catholic
Protestants and Catholics
Your Conscience as Your Guide
Jesus Christ is Lord
One God in Trinity
The Ascension of Our Lord
Heaven and Hell: A Biblical and Theological Overview

HEAVEN
AND
HELL

A Biblical and Theological Overview

PETER TOON

Thomas Nelson Publishers
Nashville • Camden • New York

For
Al and Alene Freundt in America
For
Vita and Deborah in England

Library of Congress Cataloging-in-Publication Data

Toon, Peter, 1939-
  Heaven and hell.

  1. Heaven—Biblical teaching. 2. Hell—Biblical teaching.
3. Heaven—History of doctrines. 4. Hell—History of doctrines. I. Title.
BS680.H42T66 1986   236   85-25882
ISBN 0-8407-5967-3

Contents

Preface

This book is a sequel to my *The Ascension of our Lord* (Thomas Nelson, 1984). It is not intended as a contribution to scholarly debate. Rather it is presented as a basic introductory text for students in colleges and seminaries and as a theological handbook for pastors, preachers, and teachers. In writing it I have been elated (in contemplating heaven) and deflated (in considering hell).

Working from a high view of the sacred Scriptures, I have sought to present the biblical information about heaven and hell as clearly as possible. This has been no easy task, for these realities are "outside" the space and time we know; they must be described in language which of necessity exists for communication within our space and time. Further I am not by training a biblical scholar!

Apart from the presentation of the biblical data, I have attempted to show how this was received, interpreted, and processed by Christians within the Church over the centuries since the apostolic age. Obviously I have had to be selective, and in being so I have tried to cover the major types of doctrine which have emerged as Christians have set down their understanding of heaven and hell.

The theological position of a confident belief in heaven and a reluctant belief in hell—from which I began my studies and reflections—has been strengthened by them. However, I believe that I am now far more aware than I was at the beginning of the difficulty of interpreting the imagery, symbolism, and metaphor of biblical texts. They do not easily lend themselves to being the basis for the creation of rational doctrines of what shall be after the Last Judgment.

Further, I am acutely aware that there is little teaching and preaching on heaven and hell in our churches today. I think I understand why, but I still regret the omission. I hope this book will encourage not only prayerful and careful study of these topics but also positive and informed preaching of them.

Finally, I wish to thank Paul Franklyn of Thomas Nelson for his kindness and help.

Introduction

If you believe in God the Father through Jesus Christ as your Lord and Savior, then at some time or another you will have to come to terms with your own death and what you believe there is for you (and your loved ones) beyond death. And you really cannot explore personal destiny without also reflecting upon the destiny of the universe and of the earth on which we live. The threat of nuclear war may well help to increase the urgency of reflection on these matters. As you read the Bible and recite the creeds you cannot avoid thinking about the future of the cosmos, the goal and consummation of human history, the judgment of the world by Jesus, the Christ, in the name of God, Creator and Redeemer, the criteria of that judgment and the destinies of those judged, and the new forms of reality that will be created by God to follow the Final Judgment. These topics are normally given the general title of eschatology: the doctrine of the last things.[1]

In this book we shall be making reference to them, but our main concern will be with *heaven* (understood as that which is now "above" where Christ is and also that which shall be for the righteous after the Last Judgment) and with *hell* (understood as that which exists now for the devil and evil angels and that which shall be for the wicked after the Last Judgment).

Of necessity we come to this topic as people living in western society. This context certainly affects the way we think, especially how we think about death and life after death. The questions and problems raised in our minds by our own and other people's initiatives reflect *our* culture and ethos. We are members not of a simple agrarian society but of a highly developed secularized and generally affluent society. Our cosmology is very different from that of earlier civilizations and so also is our sensitivity to the realm of the transcendent.

But as Christian believers we approach the topic with an authoritative guide as well as all kinds of helpful signposts and maps. In the sacred Scriptures we have the record of God's self-revelation; here is a unique source of information concerning heaven and hell. Then, in the history of the Christian community we have creeds, confessions, liturgies, books of theology and devotion, all of which give us important insights into the way in which the Bible has been understood in days past by people of deep spiritual insight and intellectual ability. Thus our approach is that of Anselm of Canterbury, who wrote *Credo ut intelligam* (I believe in order to understand).

And as we proceed in this spirit we need to be aware of two tendencies which have characterized some Christian thinking and often taken extreme forms. First is the spirit of philistinism which, looking solely to the glory that shall be after death and in the age to come, is blind to beauty, goodness, and harmony here on earth now within God's creation and human achievement. Second, that spirit of indifference to outward evils (even those that could be prevented) since the whole attention is given to the saving of the soul and gaining a place in heaven for it. Those who truly set their minds and hearts on the realm above where Christ is, ought like him, to be concerned about the world, its needs, and its salvation.

Let us, however, keep things in perspective. These two tendencies or dangers are minimal in importance when compared with the far greater tendency within the contemporary situation of becoming secularized in one's thinking without truly recognizing it has happened. It is so easy today to lose a genuine spiritual and moral sensitivity to the transcendent and the supernatural, which means losing sensitivity to God and his heaven. Regrettably it is rare to find a healthy attitude in seminaries, colleges, and churches today towards life after death, heaven, or hell. Our thinking and affections are earth-bound, even though we use the language of heaven and transcendence in hymns, prayers, and liturgy.

When we do seriously begin to read what the writers of the New Testament say about heaven and hell and then to explore what has been taught in the Church about these topics, we find that three important points emerge. First, the way in which the earliest Christians (as well as many after them) believed in God, Jesus Christ, and heaven is not of the same order as the way in which they have believed in Satan, devils, and hell. We place our faith in God, Jesus Christ, and heaven, but we accept the reality of Satan, the devils, and hell so as to keep far from them! It is a different logic of belief.

Second, we find that we cannot write or talk about heaven and hell from a biblical standpoint unless we accept the New Testament context for such belief. This context necessarily includes the resurrection, ascension, and session of our Lord, together with the hope of his parousia (arrival at the end of the age). Any authentic doctrine of heaven must be centered on Jesus who was raised from the dead and exalted to the right hand of the Father.

Third, much of the material in the New Testament that provides the basis for a doctrine of heaven and hell is written in apocalyptic language; e.g., the sayings of Jesus about the Parousia of the Son of Man and his judging of the peoples (e.g. Matt. 25:31ff.).[2] Though such language has a certain oddity to our ears, it had a familiar ring in the Jewish context in which Jesus lived and taught; it was natural that he should have made use of it, along with his use of the more ancient Jewish forms of speech taken from the Torah and other parts of the Hebrew Bible (our Old Testament). Of course everything he took over he transformed by his own genius and knowledge; this said, the outward form of some of his sayings is similar to those known as apocalyptic, within the Jewish literature of the period 200 BC to AD 100.[3]

Those books which are called apocalyptic usually have the following doctrinal characteristics: belief that history will not simply and evenly move from the evil age into the age of righteousness (i.e., pessimism about the progress of history); the world and the heavens as the sphere of a spiritual war between God and Satan (the chief fallen angel) for the loyalty and worship of humankind; a clear distinction between this evil age and the age of the kingdom of God which is yet to come; the imminence of the intervention of God within history to judge the wicked and reward the righteous; the expectation that the righteous dead will be raised from dead, given new bodies and made to enjoy the life of the new age after the last judgment; and the ultimate triumph of God over all his enemies, especially Satan.

Apocalyptic is best viewed as primarily but not only a development from the later prophetical books of the Old Testament canon at a time when there was a deep longing within Judaism for God to intervene on behalf of his people, to vindicate his cause, and to glorify his name (i.e., from 200 BC). Thus the authors of the apocalyptic visions, dreams and revelations use a variety of imagery, metaphor, and symbolism to communicate what they have "seen" in terms of God's heaven, the angelic hosts, the future of the righteous and the doom of the wicked. As they pull back the curtain to show aspects of the heavenly realm (e.g., God's intervention in history and the nature of his judgment of the nations), they are forced to use language to describe that with which it was never particularly designed to deal! To the modern reader much of the imagery may therefore seem bizarre and weird—just as do parts of the book of Revelation (itself called an Apocalypse) to some people today.

It is certainly true that the ethos and atmosphere of the New Testament is different from that of the Jewish apocalyptic literature. However, it is different not because Jesus and his disciples rejected apocalyptic but because they took it for granted. We must admit that had there not first developed within Judaism an apocalyptic expression of the immediate future, with the hope of an absolutely new age preceded by the resurrection of the dead, it is difficult to see how Jesus could have taught and acted in the way that he did. Jesus accepted the basic expectations of apocalyptic literature—especially the coming from heaven of the Son of Man and the resurrection of the dead, in the context of the two ages—modified or transformed them, and at the same time began to fulfill them (e.g., in his own resurrection). The apostles continued this process of development and fulfilment. Thus apocalyptic teaching forms a bridge from the Old Testament to the New Testament. It helps us to see how God began to act in Jesus in a decisive, eschatological way.

In this book there is no specific chapter on the teaching of the Old Testament books on life after death. Reference will be made to the Old Testament in most chapters, but it is excluded from the major presentation because it contains little clear and explicit teaching about heaven and hell in terms of human destiny. Certainly it has many insights into the nature of God's holy habitation which we call heaven, and we shall notice these. But apart from texts such as Psalm 73:23,24, where the psalmist reaches a particular height of inspiration and illumination, the general position of the Old Testament is to assert survival after death in the shadowy realm of Sheol.[4] Certainly at the close of the Old Testament period the belief in personal, in contrast to national, resurrection is beginning to appear (Dan. 12:2), but this belief is expressed in greater detail and with more variety in the intertestamental, apocalyptic literature.[5]

Therefore our study begins with an investigation of the teaching of Jesus concerning heaven and hell. Then we note the pivotal importance of his resurrection and ascension for the developing Christian doctrine of heaven. This leads us to study the teaching of the rest of the New Testament on heaven and hell. Having completed our biblical survey, which is part one, we turn in part two to see how the Church over the centuries has interpreted the biblical texts in creating doctrines of heaven and hell and in facing related questions. This study does not intend to provide an exhaustive study of either the biblical data or the doctrines of the Church through history. Rather the aim is to provide a reliable and interesting introduction.

Notes

[1] Etymologically, eschatology should mean "the doctrine or science of the last things" and refer to the second advent, last judgment, heaven and hell. However, in both biblical studies and systematic theology the term has been recently given a width of meaning! See further, I. H. Marshall, "Slippery Words: 1. Eschatology," *Expository Times*, Vol. 89, 1977-78, 264-69.

[2] The best book on apocalyptic is Christopher Rowland, *The Open Heaven*, London, 1982. See also D. S. Russell, *The Method and Message of Jewish Apocalyptic*, London, 1964, and *Apocalyptic: Ancient and Modern*, London, 1978. There is a helpful introduction from a conservative standpoint in S. H. Travis, *Christian Hope and the Future of Man*, Leicester, 1980.

[3] Apart from Daniel and Revelation, a list of apocalyptic writings would include the following:

1 or Ethiopic Enoch
2 or Slavonic Enoch
Jubilees
2 or Syriac Baruch

3 or Greek Baruch
4 Ezra or 2 Esdras
Apocalypse of Abraham
Testament of Abraham
Testaments of Levi and Naphtali (from the Testaments of the XII Patriarchs)
Ascension of Isaiah
Shepherd of Hermas
3 or Hebrew Enoch.

Most of these are in *The Apocryphal Old Testament*, ed. H. F. D. Sparks, Oxford University Press, 1985.

[4] For Sheol see "Dead, Abode of the" in *The Interpreter's Dictionary of the Bible*, Vol. 1, 787-89.

[5] See the article "Future Life in Intertestamental Literature" in *The Interpreter's Dictionary of the Bible*, Suppl. Vol., 348-51. For more detail see G. W. E. Nickelsburg Jr., *Resurrection, Immortality and Eternal Life in Intertestamental Judaism*, Cambridge, MA, 1972.

· PART ONE ·

Biblical Overview

·CHAPTER·
1

Proclaiming (the Kingdom of) Heaven

The primary and essential message of Jesus was that of the kingdom of heaven (God). He began his ministry by proclaiming good news about God and saying, "The time has come. The kingdom of God is near. Repent and believe the good news!" Thus it can never be said that heaven and hell were given an equivalent emphasis and value in his preaching and teaching. We shall certainly argue and assume that Jesus spoke solemnly about hell as God's provision for fallen and evil angels and that he urgently warned his hearers to repent and believe in order to avoid the possibility of going to hell. Hell is, however, a secondary feature of his teaching, not a primary one. We shall examine this teaching in the next chapter. Here we concentrate on heaven.

Since the word *heaven* has a width of meaning in the Scriptures, we shall first notice the meaning in (1) the Synoptic Gospels and (2) John's Gospel, before looking at the three themes of the kingdom of heaven, eternal life, and salvation. We do not intend to cover every reference to heaven in the Gospels; our task is to highlight the prominent features.

The term heaven

In the Old Testament heaven (Heb. *šamayim*, a plural form) often means the sky (firmament of heaven, expanse of the sky) as in Genesis 1:6ff. Here are the stars and the clouds; from here comes the dew and rain. Secondly, heaven often refers to God's unique habitation: as Solomon prayed, "Hear from heaven, your dwelling place" (1 Kings 8:30). In Hebrew cosmology this was believed to be "above" the skies, where God was served and surrounded by his heavenly host of spiritual, heavenly beings (e.g. 1 Kings 22:19ff.; Isa. 6:3ff.; Job 1:6ff.; Ps. 82:1; Dan. 7:9ff.). Even so, the Hebrews recognized that God was both above and within his creation: "The heavens, even the highest heaven, cannot contain you. How much less this temple I have built," exclaimed Solomon (1 Kings 8:27). It is from heaven, as his habitation, that God speaks to and blesses his people—as is made clear in Deuteronomy (4:36; 12:5,11 etc.). Yet neither the visible nor the invisible worlds can enclose the Lord, for not only did he create them, but he is also superior to them and does not allow them to confine him in any way.[1]

In the period between the completion of the writing of the Old Testament and the apostolic age, certain developments took place which we need to note. The tendency to avoid the use of God's name became stronger, and in its place substitutes became increasingly common, of which "heaven" was an important one. This explains, in part, the phrase "kingdom of heaven" meaning "the kingdom of God." Then, in the context of the cosmological speculations within the apocalyptic, pseudepigraphic, and rabbincal writings concerning the nature of heaven as God's holy habitation, there was a development in both the doctrine of angels and of demons.[2] Aspects of this development are reflected, as we shall note, in both the Gospels and the Epistles. Further, the belief that there will be a resurrection of the dead at the end of the age was strengthened in this period, even though it was not universally accepted in Judaism and was not expressed in one form. By his own resurrection, Jesus gave a totally new dimension to this belief: namely, that in heaven the faithful will have new, glorious bodies.

1. *Heaven in the Synoptic Gospels.* Because the aim of the Gospels is connected with God's salvation, the use of *ouranos* and *ouranoi* (which together with *ouranios*, heavenly, occur about 150 times in these three Gospels) to refer to the skies (and only the skies) is rare. For example, the birds that fly in the skies are "birds of heaven" (Matt. 6:26; 8:20). Other references which seem to mean only "sky" do, in fact, on closer examination, have an inbuilt suggestion of God's presence or habitation—e.g. Jesus lifted up his eyes to heaven (Mark 6:41). This is also true of the expression "heaven and earth" (Matt. 11:25).

The use of heaven instead of the divine name is quite common, especially in Matthew, "the Jewish Gospel." A straightforward example is provided by the question put to Jesus, "John's baptism: Was it from heaven or from men?" Here "from heaven" means "from God." Less straightforward but in the same class are the sayings about "treasure in heaven" (Matt. 6:20; Luke 12:33; Matt. 19:21; Mark 10:21; Luke 18:22), meaning treasure with God. They who do the will of God as faithful disciples of Jesus will find true riches in and with the living God, their Father in heaven. Also within this category we need to include both the "bound in heaven" and "loosed in heaven" (Matt. 16:19), meaning "before God," and "your names are written in heaven" (Luke 10:20), meaning "you are safe as held by God." The "joy in heaven" (Luke 15:7) over the repenting sinner means not only "with God" but also "with God and all the company of heaven," highlighting the community aspect of God's presence.[3]

Heaven also occurs in passages of an apocalyptic or eschatological flavor. Significantly, at the baptism of Jesus in the river Jordan by John, there is the opening of heaven (the rending of the heavens); see Mark 1:10; Matthew 3:16; Luke 3:21. Possibly the Markan text echoes the prayer of Isaiah 64:1: "Oh, that you would rend the heavens and come down"; and there are similar ideas in Jewish literature of the hearing of a voice after the rending of the heavens (see Test. Levi. 2:6; 5:1;

18:6) and of the bestowal of the Spirit (Test. Levi. 18:61ff.; Test. Jud. 24:2ff.). The Apocalypse of Baruch has these words: "Behold the heavens opened, and I saw a vision, and strength was given me, and a voice was heard from on high" (xxii. 1). The rending of the heavens points to God as Creator and Redeemer who is able to tear down and come through what he has created in order to visit his people, or in the case of Jesus, to bestow the Spirit upon the Messiah, his Chosen One.

Further, there are the references to heaven in the "little apocalypses" of Matthew 24, Mark 13 and Luke 21, and especially Matthew 24:29-31, Mark 13:24-7 and Luke 21:25-8.[4] As part of the signs associated with the coming of the Son of Man to earth from heaven at the end of this present evil age, the following phenomena are described: the stars falling from heaven, the powers in the heaven being shaken, the angels sent from heaven to gather the elect together and the sign of the Son of Man appearing in heaven. Obviously here the word heaven refers both to the habitation of God and to the extremities of the skies, and it is not necessary to separate these two meanings. There are many parallels to this form of literature within the Jewish apocalypses, and there are roots of it in the Old Testament (e.g. Isa. 13:13; 34:4; 50:3; 51:6; Jer. 4:23-6). The language used is certainly not of the same kind as that used to describe the descent of a spacecraft after its voyage in space! What it points to within its symbolic structure is (a) the sovereign power and majesty of God who initiates everything from his holy habitation, (b) the centrality of Jesus, the heavenly Son of Man, in the display of God's power, holiness and judgment of his world, and (c) the end of the present order in order to make possible a new order.

Then there are such passages as Luke 9:54; 10:18 and Mark 14:62 (// Matt. 26:64, cf. Luke 22:69). In these the apocalyptic element is obvious. In Luke 9:54 James and John ask Jesus, "Lord do you want us to call down fire from heaven to destroy them (= Samaritans)?" For this suggestion they were rebuked. Jesus knew that his glory was to be achieved via the Cross, and though he was vividly aware of the heavenly divine powers, he was also most careful about how they were used. Fire as judgment was reserved for the end time. The second Lukan text records the words of Jesus after the joyful return of the seventy disciples. He said, "I saw Satan fall like lightning from heaven." The rabbis expected the defeat of Satan and his hosts by the Messiah in the last days: Here Jesus claims that it is actually occurring in his mission and ministry in advance of the end-time. That is, Satan as the "accuser" and an angel who has rebelled against God's sovereign will has been removed from his position with the other angels in God's holy habitation. The word "lightning," which is also connected with the phenomena associated with the future coming of the Son of Man (Luke 17:24; Matt. 24:27), reflects the apocalyptic character of this saying. The final text is the reply of Jesus at his trial before the high priest to whom he said, "I am the Christ, the Son of the Blessed One, and you will see the Son of Man sitting at the right hand of the Mighty One and coming on the clouds of heaven" (Mark 14:62). Jesus appears to be quoting a combination of Daniel 7:13 and Psalm 110:1 and pointing to his enthronement as the Messiah by God and possibly to his future return to earth as judge. Thus Jesus symbolically speaks of his vindication by the Father, who will declare him truly to be the Messiah.

Note how God, as Father, is said to be in heaven—as in the Lord's Prayer (Matt. 6:9). The phrase "my Father in heaven" is found in Matthew 7:21; 10:32-33; 12:50; 16:17; 18:10,19; "my heavenly Father" in Matthew 15:13; 18:35; "your Father in heaven" in Matthew 5:16,45; 6:1; 7:11; 18:14; Mark 11:25 (cf. Luke 11:13); and "your heavenly Father" in Matthew 5:48; 6:14; 6:26; 6:32; 23:9. It is necessary to offer an explanation of the fact that in some cases the parallel verse in Mark does not have the words "Father in heaven," e.g. Matthew 12:50 and Mark 3:35, which has "the will of God" instead of "will of my Father in heaven." Instead of saying that Matthew is fond of the expression "Father in heaven" and its equivalent phrases, a better explanation is to claim that Matthew preserves the mode of speech used by Jesus and that Mark and Luke left out references to "Father in heaven" because they were conscious that Gentiles would not easily or readily understand such a description of God. To Gentiles it would imply an unworthy view of God since they would interpret the title "Father" by pagan notions of reproduction and the like.[5]

In using such a title for God as "Father in heaven," Jesus was bringing together ideas of transcendence and near presence, of sovereign majesty and personal care, of high demand and practical help. The God of the gospel is not only exalted "above" the world (i.e. remote in holiness); he is also personally involved in and with his creation, exercising tender care and requiring his children to do his will (for their good). True discipleship is life lived for and in fellowship with this God. Further, it needs to be noted that Jesus defined his own relation to this God in a different way than that of his disciples' relation to God. This difference is clear from the use of "my" and "your." The unique relation of Jesus to God is made even clearer in the Gospel of John.

2. *Heaven in John's Gospel.* Here the word occurs sixteen times (1:32; 1:51; 3:13; 3:27; 3:31; 6:31,32,33,38,41,42,50, 51,58; 12:28; 17:1), and the adjective "heavenly" once (3:12). Heaven is used as a substitute for the divine name (3:27), and there is a close identification between the physical heavens and God's holy habitation (1:32; 17:1). On most occasions heaven is used theologically of God in his holy habitation, separated from the earth; from this heaven the Son descends and to it he ascends. Let us examine several texts.

John 1:51

Jesus said, "I tell you the truth, you shall see heaven open, and the angels of God ascending and descending on the Son of Man."

This saying recalls the vision of Jacob (Gen. 28:10ff.) where there are angels and a ladder but no open heaven. The vision of the divine promised by Jesus to Nathaniel and his fellow disciples has no ladder but an open heaven. Jesus, as Son of Man, takes the place of the ladder, for it is in and through him that there is a link between heaven as God's holy habitation and earth as the place where men dwell. Jesus is the logos, the revelation of God, and the light of the world. It is important to note that the verb "open" is in the perfect tense, emphasizing that heaven is open and will remain open; fellowship with God has begun and will continue in and through the Son of Man.

In primitive apocalyptic thought the Son of Man was a heavenly being who would descend to earth from heaven on the last day to establish communion between heaven and earth. Jesus asserts that the Son of Man has already come and heaven is open; eternal life is now freely available as the gift of God (see below on eternal life).[6]

John 3:12-13

> Jesus said, "I have spoken to you of earthly things and you do not believe; how then will you believe if I speak of heavenly things? No-one has ever gone into heaven except the one who came from heaven—the Son of Man."

The "earthly things" are probably events in the physical realm such as birth and wind (to which reference has been made earlier in John 3), which point parabolically to the gospel, Christ, and the work of the Spirit. Jesus has used parables to encourage true faith in Nicodemus, but these have not yet achieved their purpose. Thus it will be useless for Jesus to speak directly without illustrations of "heavenly things," spiritual realities. It is not possible, Jesus continues, for men to mount up to heaven and attain direct knowledge of God by visiting him in his holy habitation. As the heavenly Son of Man he has come from God and by his incarnation has made himself (and thus heavenly things) accessible to earthly men. Thus Jesus is the key to true knowledge of God and participation in his life, the gift of eternal life. Heaven is from where Jesus comes and to where he goes.

John 6:38 and 51

> Jesus said, "For I have come down from heaven not to do my will but to do the will of him (my Father) who sent me . . . I am the living bread that came down from heaven. If a man eats of this bread he will live forever."

Again heaven is from where Jesus comes to be incarnate among men. The purpose of his coming is to do the will of the Father (thus his "It is finished" on the cross (19:30)) and as part of this to provide eternal life (living bread) for those who receive him as Messiah. That he has come down from God in heaven is repeated seven times in this chapter—verses 33,38,41,42,50,51,58. Further it is also stated in this chapter that the will of God includes the resurrection of faithful believers "at the last day" (39-40).

What Jesus proclaimed and provided as the gift of God to repentant and believing sinners is described in the four gospels as entering the kingdom of heaven (God), receiving eternal life, and being saved. The account of the visit of the rich young man to Jesus (Mark 10:17-31; Matthew 19:16-30; Luke 18:18-30) reveals that these heavenly provisions are dynamically equivalent.[7]

The young man asked what he had to do to "inherit eternal life"; Jesus told him that apart from obeying the commandments he had to sell all that he possessed, give to the poor, and become a disciple. Seeing that this reply did not please the rich young man, Jesus commented that it is hard for those with riches to "enter the kingdom of God." Somewhat surprised by this reply, the disciples then asked whether anyone could "be saved." Jesus told them that with God all things are possible and that those who make genuine sacrifice for his (Jesus') sake will receive "eternal life in the age to come."

To inherit eternal life, to enter the kingdom of God, and to be saved are different ways of expressing the relationship to God of a person who is united to Jesus in faith and discipleship. Though their meanings are not strictly identical, they point to the one divine reality which God brings into being by his power through the Gospel.

It will now be our task to look at these three themes in the teaching of Jesus. As we proceed we shall bear in mind that the Parousia (the arrival in glory of Jesus as Son of Man) and the final judgment mark the division temporally between this evil age and the future age of the kingdom of heaven/God, when salvation will be completed and eternal life enjoyed. Further, we shall bear in mind that, in contrast with some Jewish apocalyptic sources, Jesus is reticent concerning conditions of life after his Parousia. However, what he does teach is sufficient for us to grasp the feelings of the apostle Paul who, recalling Isaiah 64:3, wrote "No eye has seen, no ear heard, no mind has conceived what God has prepared for those who love him" (1 Cor. 2:9).

The kingdom of heaven/God[8]

It is necessary to provide a few examples to show that the kingdom of God is synonymous with the kingdom of heaven. This can be done by placing side by side parallel texts from Matthew (who uses "kingdom of heaven") and both Mark and Luke.

> Mark 1:15 The time has come. The Kingdom of God is near. Repent . . .
> Matt. 4:17 Repent for the kingdom of heaven is near.

11

Matt. 11:11 He who is least in the kingdom of heaven is greater than he [John].

Luke 7:28 The one who is least in the kingdom of God is greater than he.

Mark 4:11 The secret of the kingdom of God has been given to you.

Matt. 13:11 The knowledge of the secrets of the kingdom of heaven has been given to you.

(Others include Matt. 5:3 // Luke 6:20, Matt. 13:33 // Luke 13:20, and Matt. 19:14 // Mark 10:14 and Luke 18:16.)

By way of general observations, it is generally accepted by New Testament scholars that the teaching of Jesus concerning the kingdom refers to the gracious reign of God both in the present and in the future and that the kingdom includes both. But precisely how Jesus himself saw the relation of future and present is not easy to determine or state. Jesus never formally defined the expression "kingdom of God," nor did he distinguish his usage from that of his contemporaries, be they rabbis or Essenes. Certainly, in line with the prophets of Israel he looked for the total implementation of God's gracious reign in terms of a new creation in which people were united to their Lord in a new covenant. This new order would follow the "day of the Lord," an event he described in apocalyptic terms and with reference to himself as the Judge. But he also spoke and lived as one whose own ministry actually brought God's gracious and liberating reign into human lives as he enabled people to become whole and to enjoy genuine fellowship and communion with God as Father.

Various analogies may help us understand how a kingdom that will certainly be is already truly present. The kingdom of the present is like the dawning of a new day; it is the real day but only the first intimation and experience of it. Or the kingdom of the present is like the tip of the iceberg; the real thing but only a small part of the total reality. Or the kingdom of the present is like the firstfruits of the harvest, the initial deposit before the final payment is made, and the honeymoon at the beginning of a marriage. So it is said that the kingdom is not yet in its fullness but is already here in its initial impact.

In teaching about the kingdom Jesus used many parables.[9] These are forms of speech which create comparisons between commonplace objects, events, and persons (e.g., harvest, fish, weddings, children) and a less common reality (e.g., the reality of the kingdom of God). The parables of Jesus certainly effect a comparison between the earthly and the heavenly (transcendent). It is important to remember this when they relate to heaven and hell. Parabolic teaching is sometimes allegorical, even though some of it amounts to short stories. None of the parables which deal with life *after* the final judgment are allegorical.

Before we look at those parables which deal with the heavenly life of the age to come, we must quickly notice those sayings and parables of Jesus which indicate (1) that the kingdom is a present reality, the dawning of the age of salvation, and (2) the certainty of future judgment before the complete arrival of the kingdom.

1. Three sayings of Jesus point to his conviction that *the kingdom had dawned* or come near *through his presence* and ministry.

Luke 17:20-21

> Once, having been asked by the Pharisees when the kingdom of God would come, Jesus replied, "The kingdom of God does not come visibly, nor will people say, 'Here it is', or 'There it is', because the kingdom of God is within (or, among) you."

The question from the Pharisees presupposed the apocalyptic conviction that the arrival of the kingdom can be calculated in terms of specific external signs—wars, earthquakes, etc.

13

Jesus tells them that in looking for a future kingdom they were overlooking the presence of the kingdom in his person and ministry. The Greek *entos* can be translated "within," "among," or "in the midst of."

Matthew 12:28

> If I cast out demons by the Spirit of God, surely the kingdom of God has come upon you (NKJV cf. Luke 11:20).

The exorcisms by Jesus and his binding of Satan point to the arrival of the kingdom of God and the overthrow of the king- dom of Satan.

Matthew 11:12-13

> From the days of John the Baptist until now, the kingdom of heaven has been forcefully advancing, and forceful men lay hold of it. For all the Prophets and the Law prophesied until John. (cf. Luke 16:16).

This is not an easy statement to interpret, but it is clear that the ministry of John the Baptist was seen by Jesus as the end- ing of the old period of revelation which includes the prophets and the law. With Jesus and his ministry a new era, a new period, the time of the kingdom has come and has been advancing against the domain of Satan.

2. Since the theme of the day of the Lord's judgment was emphasized by both the canonical prophets and apocalyptic writers it is not surprising that *Jesus also had much to say about judgment.* Among the parables are those of the Weeds (Matt. 13:24-30), the Unmerciful Servant (Matt. 18:23-34) the Ten Maidens (Matt. 25:1-12), the Doorkeeper (Mark 13:34) and the Thief (Matt. 24:43), and the eschatological discourse of Matthew 25:31-46.

For the righteous there will be fellowship with Jesus in the heavenly life of the age to come. This is conveyed through the image of the banquet. We must now examine how this image is used.

Matthew 8:11 (// Luke 13:29)

> Jesus said, "I say to you that many will come from the east and the west and will take their places at the feast with Abraham, Isaac and Jacob in the kingdom of heaven."

In the tradition of the rabbis Jesus spoke of the new quality and depth of life in the age to come through the picture of a banquet or marriage feast. We must bear in mind that such occasions and meals were much looked forward to and highly valued by people who worked hard, for long hours and possessed few luxuries. Not only the food but the communal celebration was enjoyed.

Isaiah had spoken of the future reign of God in this way: "On this mountain the LORD Almighty will prepare a feast of rich food for all peoples, a banquet of aged wine—the best of meats and the finest of wines" (25:6). Here God is presented as preparing a great banquet on Mount Zion to celebrate his enthronement as King. It is a sumptuous banquet with a universal invitation for all people, Jew and Gentile.

From this image the idea of the messianic banquet developed, to which reference is made in the apocryphal writings. For example, 'Rise, stand up, and see the whole company of those who bear the Lord's mark and sit at his table. They have moved out of the shadow of this world and have received shining robes from the Lord' (2 Esdras 2:38-9; see also from Qumran 1QSa. 2:11-21). The messianic age and the age of the kingdom were pictured as beginning with banquets of food more delicious than the manna provided by God in the wilderness for Moses and Israel.

Thus Jesus taught that in the heavenly age to come Jews

and Gentiles will live in joy and in fellowship with the Lord and each other.

Luke 12:37

> Jesus said, "It will be good for those servants whose master finds them watching when he comes. I tell you the truth, he will dress himself to serve, will have them recline at table and will come and wait on them."

This is part of a parable told by Jesus in order to emphasize the need for watchfulness by his disciples as they awaited his Parousia. In the parable the master, on his return, reverses roles; he dresses himself as a servant and prepares a banquet for his faithful servants. By this image Jesus again points to the superabundant blessings of God's grace in the new age of the kingdom.

Luke 16:9

> Jesus said, "I tell you, use worldly wealth to gain friends for yourself, so that when it is gone, you will be welcomed into eternal dwellings."

Disciples are to use their money and possessions in the service of the kingdom to gain, as it were, the friendship of God and his good angels in order that they will then welcome them into God's holy habitation, where the angels adore him. This recalls the teaching of Jesus in John 14:2. "In my Father's house are many rooms; if it were not so I would have told you. I am going there to prepare a place for you."

Luke 22:29-30 (cf. Matt. 19:28)

> Jesus said, "I confer on you a kingdom, just as my Father conferred one on me, so that you may eat and drink at my table in my kingdom and sit on thrones, judging the twelve tribes of Israel."

Here Jesus makes a promise to those disciples who have continued with him over the last three years in his trials. The verb "to confer" used here is normally used with reference to the making of a covenant by God: Thus the glorious future to which he looks forward is as sure as the covenant of God. In this they will share with their Lord the task of governing and ruling the new people of God (Israel). Probably Jesus has in mind their pivotal position in the creation of the Church and its early organization in which they will be engaged before enjoying the fullness of the banquet of the kingdom of the age to come.

Matthew 19:28 has the word *palingenesia* (renewal, regeneration of all things) pointing to the cosmic renewal involved in the theme of the kingdom.

Matthew 22:1-14

> The kingdom of heaven is like a king who prepared a wedding banquet for his son . . .

This is the parable of the wedding banquet (cf. Luke 14:16-24). Jesus uses the image of the feast to convey the joyous fellowship and communion of the coming heavenly age of the kingdom as well as to warn the Jews of their exclusion if they do not repent and receive the Gospel. The coming kingdom will be God's eschatological table of sharing involving Jew and Gentile.

Matthew 25:1-13

> The virgins who were ready went in with the bridegroom to the wedding banquet.

The parable of the ten virgins emphasized the need for watchfulness in terms of the Parousia, which will be followed by the great banquet to which all the faithful and watchful will be invited. They will attend and rejoice in the celebration of the union of God and his people.

Mark 14:25 (// Matt. 26:29; Luke 22:18)

> Jesus said, "I tell you the truth, I will not drink again of the fruit of the vine until that day when I drink it anew in the kingdom of God."

This statement was made at the Last Supper in the context of the Passover meal. "That day" points to the Parousia of Jesus as Son of Man, to be followed by the establishment of perfect and uninterrupted fellowship between God and his covenant people in the experience of the salvation brought by Jesus as Messiah. The cup that Jesus did not drink was probably the fourth cup used in the Passover ritual; it was associated with the promise that God will take his people to be with him forever (Exod. 6:6-7).[10]

In these texts the image of the banquet is clear, pointing to the final consummation of the kingdom, in which there will be celebration, joy, and communion/fellowship of a super-abundant and amazing quality. Because it will be of this nature, the future heavenly kingdom will also be a sphere of enlarged opportunities for the righteous in their service of God. This is communicated in those parables of Jesus where servants are placed in charge of greater possessions/lands following faithful service (e.g., Luke 12:44; Matt. 24:47; Luke 19:17,19).

Two further characteristics of the future heavenly kingdom deserve notice. First, it is characterized by being absolutely *new*, and secondly, its members are truly blessed. The new wine cannot be put into old wineskins, for the God who says, "I am doing a new thing." (Isa. 43:19), is creating a new order in and through the Messiah. At his Parousia, said Jesus, there would be the "renewal of all things" (Matt. 19:28). This dimension of newness is expressed in what Jesus told the Sadducees about the Resurrection: "When the dead rise, they will neither marry nor be given in marriage; they will be like the angels in heaven" (Mark 12:25; Matt. 22:30; Luke 20:34-36). Contrary to the common Jewish idea that earthly relationships in a purer and deeper form would be resumed after the resurrection, Jesus teaches that it will be a new creation, not merely the reinstatement of the original one. It is probably because it will be absolutely new that Jesus never tried to represent it graphically. Whatever precisely it will be like, its center will be harmony and communion with God through the Son.[11]

After the judgment the Son of Man will say to the sheep on his right hand: "Come, you who are blessed by my Father; take your inheritance, the kingdom prepared for you since the creation of the world" (Matt. 25:34). Here Jesus is saying that God, the Father, has pronounced blessing (*eulogomēnos* = *barak* in the Old Testament and indicates the blessedness which belongs to God as God) upon the righteous so that they truly are "the blessed of the Blest." In the Beatitudes of Matthew 5 and Luke 6 the word translated "blessed" is *makarios* and means "Oh the happiness of," indicating fullness of joy from the human recipient's point of view. It is in the second half of the Beatitudes that the nature of true blessedness is delineated and what it means to be "the blessed of the Blest" is explored. It is *eulogemēnos* which in its fullness belongs to the future kingdom even though it is actually experienced now in part by those who trust in God, receive the Messiah, and do the divine will. As a ray of light passes through a prism to be broken up into the colors of the rainbow, so the reality of the kingdom for the faithful is expressed in the colorful promises of the Beatitudes. The righteous and faithful who already know the rule of God in their hearts will experience the perfection of that rule; they who now know the comfort of God will experience the elimination of all pain and suffering with genuine peace and tranquility; they who now long for a right relationship with God and their fellow men will experience such an in-depth relationship with God in Christ and in the communion of saints; they who now experience divine mercy and are merciful will know the experience of the full reception and appropriation of the divine mercy; and they who now seek to have singleness of mind and purity of heart will be granted the *visio dei*, the sight of God in the face of Jesus Christ by the power of the Holy Spirit. So we see that the blessedness is eschatological but not expressed in apocalyptic terminology; experienced now, it will be known constantly and fully in the new divine order of the kingdom of heaven.

Eternal Life

The rich young man asked, "What must I do to inherit eternal life?" (Mark 10:17). His attitude reflected current Jewish piety, a piety of achievement (cf. Pss. Solomon 14:6; 3:16; 14:10; 1 Enoch 38:4; 40:9; 48:3; 2 Macc. 7:9). Jesus spoke of *receiving*, as a gift, eternal life. Although the expression "eternal life" is not common in the Synoptic Gospels, occurring only seven times, the word "life" is sometimes used in such a way as to have the same meaning as "eternal life." For example, "It is better for you to enter into *life* maimed than with two hands to go into hell" (Mark 9:43; cf. Matt. 7:14; Acts 3:15; 5:20; 11:18).

The function of "eternal" (*aionios*), which literally means "pertaining to an age," is to give a quantitative definition to the qualitative life, received as God's gift. It is the life of the age that begins after the Last Judgment and which has no end. And that which is properly a future blessing becomes a present fact in virtue of the realization of the future in Jesus, the Messiah. The possession of the gift of eternal life through belief in the Messiah in this age as an anticipation of its full possession in the age to come is a theme much emphasized in John's Gospel. In this "spiritual" gospel eternal life is always presented as the gift of God to the believer: Neither the Father nor the Son are said to have it since the Father "has life in himself" (5:26) and he has granted this same life to the Son (5:26).

In his Prologue, John told his readers that "in the Word was life and that life was the light of men." Life (*zoē*) and light (*phōs*) go together; he who has life is the Revealer of deity. The Word made flesh, the Son and the Messiah, is the life (11:25; 14:6), the bread of life (6:35,48), the light of life (8:12), who gives the water of life (4:10f; 7:38) and bread of life (6:50ff.). His words are spirit and life (6:63) and actual words of eternal life (6:68). And this life (*zoē*) cannot be put to death, for when Jesus dies upon the Cross it is his mortal life (*psychē*) which he gives up in death.[12]

To receive the incarnate Son and to believe in him results in the bestowal of revelation and of eternal life (3:16). It is noteworthy that eternal life is first mentioned in the gospel immediately after the sole reference to the kingdom of God (3:3,5). Thus the Johannine emphasis upon eternal life as a gift present that anticipates a greater fullness in the age to come, resembles the synoptic emphasis upon God's saving rule coming into human lives now. In fact a study of the seventeen references to eternal life show that while reference to the age to come is retained, it is not prominent (3:15,16,36; 4:14,36; 5:24,39; 6:27,40,47,54,68; 10:28; 12:25,50; 17:2,3). Eternal life is presented as a quality and depth of life given by God to believers in this age that they might truly know him in this age and the age to come.

The truth that eternal life is received in the present is clear from such a statement of Jesus' as this: "I tell you the truth, whoever hears my word and believes him who sent me has eternal life and will not be condemned; he has crossed over from death to life" (5:24). However, the future gaining of life is made clear in this promise made to the woman at the well: "Whoever drinks the water I give him will never thirst. Indeed the water I give him will become in him a spring of water welling up to eternal life" (4:14; see also 4:36; 5:28; 6:27; 12:25).

If the primary characteristic of the possession of eternal life now is genuine knowledge of God and communion with him in the life of faith/faithfulness, then to what do the believing faithful look forward? In his priestly prayer recorded in John 17, Jesus prayed: "Father, I want those you have given me to be with me where I am, and to see my glory, the glory you have given me because you loved me before the creation of the world" (v. 24). To be present with Christ and to have fellowship with him in the sphere of his glorified Being constitute a much deeper and more profound experience of grace than the highest moments of spiritual fellowship on earth in this age. The glory of the exalted Jesus is the radiance of the eternal deity that he shares with the Father in the unity of the Holy Trinity. The final wish of Jesus was that his disciples be with him, in his true home, the Father's presence; there they will "see his glory," not with human physical eyes but with the eyes of the heart and understanding and be lost in wonder, love, and praise (cf. 2 Cor. 3:18 and 1 John 3:2). In the Old Testament glory refers not to God in his essential nature but to God in self-unveiling and self-revelation, especially in his mighty acts of salvation (Exod. 14:17ff.; Ps. 96:3). Because Jesus is the incarnate Son of God, he radiates God's glory but does so in such a way that his followers (with whom he shares human nature) are enabled by grace to enjoy the power and blessing of the self-unveiling of God in and through him.

Eternal life, a present possession, will be a future reality also and will include being with Jesus for ever and seeing the glory of God in him.

Salvation[13]

After the rich young man had gone away sorrowful, Jesus told the disciples: "Children, how hard it is to enter the kingdom of God! It is easier for a camel to pass through the eye of a needle than for a rich man to enter the kingdom of God." This statement amazed the disciples who asked, "Who then can be saved?" (Mark 10:24,26). Jesus explained that with God the impossible is possible and that men can and will be saved.

To appreciate this reference to salvation from God we need to recall that salvation is an important theme in the later prophetic teaching of the Old Testament, where it is presented as a new creation: that is, the old creation renewed by God's redemption. The hope of a new Israel in a new environment is implicit in the concept of God's salvation which has three strands. The oldest strand is the renewal of the natural order, a restoration of the original, paradisal condition (Isa. 9:2-7; 11:1-9). Then there is the provision of the new political order, wherein all nations bring their gifts to Jerusalem and Israel is truly a light to the nations (49:5-13). Finally, there is the vision of the new cosmic order of new heavens and earth (65:17; 66:22).

For the full development of the concepts of the resurrection of the body and of rewards and punishments after death, we have to leave the Old Testament and go into the intertestamental literature. Jesus made use of this development as he also revived the idea of salvation as a new creation wrought by divine grace. In fact the name, Jesus, means "The Lord is salvation." And Simeon, after seeing Jesus as a babe, exclaimed, "My eyes have seen your salvation" (Luke 2:30). In this child, born in Bethlehem, Simeon perceived the beginning and also the center of God's new creation since this child is both "a light for revelation to the Gentiles and for glory to your people Israel" (2:32).

As he began his ministry Jesus proclaimed that salvation came to an individual and a household when one embraced and received the gospel of the kingdom. After Zaccheus, the tax-collector, expressed his intention to live by the gospel, Jesus declared: "Today salvation has come to this house because this man, too, is a son of Abraham. For the Son of Man came to seek and save what was lost" (Luke 19:9-10). To receive salvation a person had to repent and believe in the God who is revealed in the gospel of the kingdom. Jesus told the woman "who was a sinner" that her faith had saved her; in her life a new creation had occurred as her sins had been forgiven (see Luke 7:36-50).

For Jesus salvation meant the forgiveness of sins, the healing of the body/mind/spirit, the making whole of the person, and the participation in the new creation through the gift of eternal life and membership of the kingdom of God/heaven. Therefore, salvation is both a present and a future reality: In fact it is a present reality because as a future reality it has been brought into the present in the life and ministry of Jesus, the Messiah. And though salvation is a gift from God, it does make demands upon its recipients. Thus on one occasion Jesus said: "He who stands firm to the end will be saved" (Mark 13:13; Matt. 10:22; 24:13). Salvation means being placed by God in the new creation coming into being in and around the Messiah, a creation that anticipates the fullness and joy of the complete salvation yet to come.

What the apostles preached is well summarized in Acts 4:12: "Salvation is found in no-one else, for there is no other name under heaven given to men by which we must be saved." And the apostle Paul spoke of this salvation in terms of new creation (Gal. 6:15), while Peter said that "we are looking forward to a new heaven and new earth, the home of righteousness" (2 Pet. 3:13).

Conclusion

Heaven is the place and sphere where God is wholly and

specially known and experienced by his adoring creatures as they serve him. Heaven will be "enlarged" after the resurrection of the incarnate Son, for creatures will see the glory of God in and through this Son. Further, the kingdom of heaven of the age to come after the final judgment of the nations will be a new creation with God in Christ at its center, surrounded by a community who have eternal life, whose sins have been forgiven and who, being pure in heart, see God. This new creation will know no misery or pain but will be filled with joy, peace, and righteousness as its members, in their resurrection bodies, grow deeper into the experience of the mercy of God.

Most of the teaching of Jesus concerning life after death had reference to the kingdom of heaven after his own Parousia and judgment of the nations. But, it may be asked, did he say anything about disciples going to heaven at their death, in the period between his Ascension and Parousia? It is quite possible that he expected that his Parousia would occur very soon after his Exaltation into heaven. We shall never know the answer to this problem because the language of apocalyptic is the language of imminence and urgency. Since Jesus used this language to speak of his Parousia, it was inevitable that some of his sayings gave the impression of an imminent return in glory.[14] However, people die every day, and even if he had returned quickly, some would have died between the Exaltation and Parousia. So this is a legitimate question to ask. Two texts merit attention.

First of all there are the familiar words of John 14:1-3: "Do not let your hearts be troubled. Trust in God; trust also in me. In my Father's house are many rooms; if it were not so I would have told you. I am going there to prepare a place for you. And if I go and prepare a place for you I will come back and take you to be with me that you also may be where I am." "My Father's house" is a way of describing heaven as God's holy habitation, where there are sufficient rooms for all the righteous (as the apocalyptic writers had explained: 1 Enoch 39:4; 41:2; 45:3; 2 Esdras 7:80,101). Jesus, as the Messiah, is to go ahead of his people to prepare their heavenly and eternal habitations (cf. Luke 16:9). And he will return to them in the presence and power of the Paraclete (Holy Spirit) and also in his Parousia. Thus the taking back to heaven may refer to both the taking in and through death and in triumph at his Parousia. However, the primary emphasis appears to be on the latter rather than the former.[15]

In the second place there are the words of Jesus from the Cross: "I tell you the truth, today you will be with me in paradise" (Luke 23:43). These words were addressed to the penitent thief. Was Jesus saying that at his death he would enter into heaven? Paradise is a Persian word meaning a walled park or garden. It was taken over into both Hebrew and Greek. In the Septuagint it was used of the Garden of Eden and then, because of the Jewish belief that God would bring the restoration of the primeval bliss of Eden, paradise became the word to describe the future abode of the righteous in the age to come and, to a lesser extent, the intermediate state of bliss between death and the birth of the age of the kingdom. Thus it is possible Jesus was telling the penitent thief that as a disembodied spirit he would enter paradise to await for the complete paradise of the kingdom of heaven.

But there is another way of interpreting the promise of Jesus.

"Today" may be taken as referring to the great saving event begun on Good Friday and ending in the Resurrection, Ascension, and exaltation of Jesus into heaven. "Today" is the "time of messianic salvation." If this is so, the thief is being told that by believing in Jesus he is united to him and that he will be exalted with him as a member of his body into heaven. Therefore his salvation is sure for the age to come.[16]

It would seem that there is no absolutely clear teaching of Jesus concerning the "intermediate state." Even the parable of the rich man and Lazarus does not easily lend itself to providing clarity on this point. The focus of that parable is the self-pandering unbelief of the five brothers (Luke 16:27-31). The paradisal state of reclining on Abraham's bosom may point only to the kingdom of heaven of the age to come. For Jesus the hope of the disciple was to focus on the Parousia and the kingdom to come.

Notes

[1] For the Old Testament presentation of heaven see Ulrich Simon, *Heaven in the Christian Tradition*, London, 1958, chapters 1-4.

[2] See further W. G. E. Nickelsburg, Jr. *Resurrection, Immortality and Eternal Life in Intertestamental Judaism*.

[3] See further William Strawson, *Jesus and the Future Life*, London, 1959, 36-37.

[4] See the comments of William L. Lane, *The Gospel of Mark*, Grand Rapids, 1974, 444ff. and the authorities and studies cited there.

[5] This is the suggestion of G. Dalman, *The Words of Jesus* (E. T. D. M. Kay), Edinburgh, 1902, 190-92.

[6] See further C. Rowland, *The Open Heaven*, 178ff., and C. K. Barrett, *The Gospel according to St. John*, London, 1967, 156.

[7] Cf. the exposition by William L. Lane, *Mark*, 362ff.

[8] There are many studies of the theme of the kingdom of God. See e.g., Joachim Jeremias, *New Testament Theology*, Vol. 1, London 1971, 76ff. and Leonhard Goppelt, *Theology of the New Testament*, Vol. 1, London, 1981, 43ff. A comprehensive treatment is John Gray, *The Biblical Doctrine of the Reign of God*, Edinburgh, 1979, and a simpler introduction is A. M. Hunter, *Christ and the Kingdom*, Edinburgh, 1980.

[9] See further Joachim Jeremias, *The Parables of Jesus*, New York, 1963.

[10] For more detail see Lane, *Mark*, 508.

[11] Cf. L. Goppelt, *Theology*, 73; J. Jeremias, *Theology*, 248.

[12] I have found the commentaries of C. K. Barrett (1978[2]), R. E. Brown (1966, 1970, 2 vols.) and L. Morris (1970) very helpful for their explanation of the theme of life and light.

[13] For the theme of salvation in the Bible, see under "Redemp-

tion" in the *New International Dictionary of New Testament Theology*, Vol. 3, Grand Rapids, MI, 177-221.

[14] S. H. Travis comments that "the imminence language of Jesus asserts that the age of the decisive fulfillment has really dawned, the kingdom of God is being manifested here and now, and the present manifestations guarantee God's ultimate triumph through Christ," *Christian Hope*, 90.

[15] R. H. Gundry argues that *monai* (rooms) are spiritual positions in Christ; see his "In my Father's House are many *Monai*," *Zeitschrift für die Neutestamentliche Wissenschaft*, Vol. 58, 1967, 68ff.

[16] E. E. Ellis, *The Gospel of Luke*, London, 1974², 268-69.

·CHAPTER·
2

Warnings Concerning Hell

We have already claimed that heaven and hell did not have an equivalent weight or logical position in the teaching of Jesus. Bearing this in mind we shall examine the recorded words of Jesus that directly or indirectly refer to hell as they are found in (a) Mark, (b) the material common to Matthew and Luke, (c) Matthew alone, (d) Luke alone, and (e) John alone. Further, we shall briefly note the recorded statement of John the Baptist on this topic.

Mark

In this, the first of the Gospels, we read of the possibility of committing an eternal sin, of being lost, of the Son of Man being ashamed of certain people at his Parousia, and of Gehenna (hell) itself.

3:28-9 (// Matt. 12:31-2; Luke 12:10)

> I tell you the truth, all the sins and blasphemies of men will be forgiven them. But whoever blasphemes against the Holy Spirit will never be forgiven; he is guilty of an eternal sin.

An "eternal sin" is an odd expression and probably means a sin so serious as to have eternal consequences. Jesus did not say that the scribes had already committed this sin; but he was

warning that they were in danger of committing it by their
persistent refusal to recognize the work of God in his ministry
as the Messiah of Israel. Not ever to be forgiven by God, the
Creator and Judge, is a frightening state.

8:34-8 (// Matt. 16:24-8; Luke 9:23-7)

> If anyone will come after me, he must deny himself and take up
> his cross and follow me. For whoever wants to save his life will
> lose it, but whoever loses his life for me and for the gospel will
> save it. What good is it for a man to gain the whole world, yet
> forfeit his soul? Or what can a man give in exchange for his soul?
> If anyone is ashamed of me and my words in this adulterous gen-
> eration, the Son of Man will be ashamed of him when he comes
> in his Father's glory with the holy angels.

Jesus called for radical discipleship in new life. Its opposite is
life dominated by the sinful self, its motivations and aspira-
tions, whose end is perdition. Life without Christ is life that is
for this age only. It is to be lost.[1]

Further, to be ashamed of Jesus, the Messiah, in this world
will ensure that when he returns to earth as Son of Man and
Judge, he will likewise be ashamed of (judge adversely) those
who have rejected him on earth. Both the loss of eternal life
and the adverse judgment of the Son of Man point to exclusion from God's holy presence in the age to come.

9:42-8 (// Matt. 18:6-9; Luke 17:1-2; Matt. 5:29-30)

> And if anyone causes one of these little ones who believe in me
> to sin, it would be better for him to be thrown into the sea with a
> large millstone tied around his neck. If your hand causes you to
> sin, put it off. It is better for you to enter life maimed than with
> two hands to go into hell, where the fire never goes out. And if
> your foot causes you to sin, cut it off. It is better for you to enter
> life crippled than to have two feet and be thrown into hell. And
> if your eye causes you to sin, pluck it out. It is better for you to
> enter the kingdom of God with one eye than to have two eyes

and be thrown into hell, Where their worm does not die and the fire is not quenched.

Here are some very serious warnings uttered by Jesus as he made use of the familiar picture of Gehenna (rendered "hell" here and elsewhere).[2] The general point of them is that it is worth making costly sacrifices for the sake of not losing the gift of eternal life. Gehenna was the valley west of Jerusalem where at one time children were sacrificed to the god, Moloch (see 2 Kings 23:10; Jer. 7:31; 19:5ff.). It was desecrated by king Josiah and then used as the garbage dump for the city of Jerusalem; this fact explains the use of the imagery of worm and maggots, cited from Isaiah 66:24. The picture is of worms and maggots crawling and living off offal, together with fires perpetually smoldering and burning as more refuse is tipped on the site.

In Jewish thought, particularly apocalyptic thought, Gehenna had come to convey the concept of a place of torment for the wicked, following God's holy judgment of them. For example in 1 Enoch we read: "Then Raphael, one of the holy angels . . . said to me, 'This accursed valley is for those who are cursed for ever; here will be gathered together all who speak with their mouths against the Lord . . . and here will be their place of judgement.'," (1 Enoch 27:2. Cf. 90:26ff. and 4 Ezra 7:36; 2 Baruch 59:10, 85:13).

Recalling that the Lord has "a fire in Zion and a furnace in Jerusalem" (Isa. 31:9) and that there is a place of cursing near to Jerusalem where the inhabitants of the city go "to look upon the dead bodies of those who rebelled against" the Lord and where "their worm will not die, nor will their fire be quenched" (Isa. 66:24), it is easy to understand how this valley came to be the image of the place of eternal punishment in apocalyptic thought.

Material Common to Matthew and Luke

In these texts we have references to God's wrath, fire, Hades, Gehenna, prison, destruction, and rejection.

Matthew 3:7 // Luke 3:7

> John said to the Pharisees and Sadducees: You brood of vipers! Who warned you to flee from the coming wrath? Produce fruit in keeping with repentance.

John's baptism was a single, unrepeatable act, with no ritual significance, and it is not to be confused with the Qumran rites. David Hill writes:

> The scrolls of the Qumran sect add to our knowledge of the wider background of John's movement, but there is no evidence that John himself belonged to such a group; he emerged from such a milieu, and that is the most that can be claimed. In its unique character, its availability (as moral purification) to all, and its preparing for an imminent eschatological baptism in spirit and fire, the Johannine rite demonstrates a profound originality which may be due to reflection on the prophetic demand for purity and righteousness of life before the judgment of God (Isa. 1:16).[3]

Thus the wrath from which to flee is that of the final judgment, the great "day of the LORD," when the wicked and unrepentant will incur the divine displeasure and punishment.

Matthew 3:12 // Luke 3:17

> John said: "His winnowing fork is in his hand, and he will clear his threshing floor, gathering wheat into his barn and burning up the chaff with unquenchable fire."

Here John predicts that the coming of the Messiah will involve judgment involving destruction and punishment. The winnowing fork is used to throw corn and chaff into the air where the wind separates them; thus the threshing floor is cleansed of the chaff. The Messiah will separate the repentant from the unrepentant, gathering the former into his

kingdom and condemning the latter to punishment. The unquenchable fire is an image used in the prophetic literature
(see Isa. 34:10; 66:24; Jer. 7:20) to point to adverse judgment
and punishment from the Lord, and it was used in apocalyptic
literature and by the rabbis.[4]

Matthew 5:25-6 // Luke 12:57-9

> Settle matters quickly with your adversary who is taking you to
> court. Do it while you are still with him on the way, or he may
> hand you over to the judge, and the judge may hand you over to
> the officer, and you may be thrown into prison. I tell you the
> truth, you will not get out until you have paid the last penny.

Apart from the direct application of this teaching to the practical situations in which disciples find themselves, there is an
allegorical interpretation which points to the necessity of being reconciled to God while there is still time in this life before the accuser (Satan? the Law?) arraigns you before God as
Judge. In both Isaiah 24:21-2 and 2 Enoch 13:24 the place to
which the wicked pass at death is called a prison or dungeon;
the last penny is *quadrans*, an exceedingly small sum. Thus
this sombre warning from Jesus concerns the consequences of
failing to be in the right with God.

Matthew 7:13-4; Luke 13:23-4

> Enter through the narrow gate. For wide is the gate and broad is
> the road that leads to destruction, and many enter through it.
> But small is the gate and narrow the road that leads to life, and
> only a few find it.

The idea of the two ways is found in the Old Testament (see
Deut. 30:19 and Jer. 21:8) and in Jewish writings (4 Ezra
7:7ff.; Test. Asher. 1:3,5; P. Aboth ii. 12-3). "Destruction"
refers to the reception of adverse judgment by the Lord at the

end of the age; it is the opposite of being given the gift of eternal life. In the Apocalypse of Esdras there is a description of a visit to Tartarus/Gehenna which includes these words: "And they led me down to the bottom of the pit of destruction, and I saw there the twelve plagues of the abyss" (iv, 21-2).

Matthew 8:11-2; Luke 13:27-8

> I say to you that many will come from the east and the west, and will take their places at the feast with Abraham, Isaac, and Jacob in the kingdom of heaven. But the subjects of the kingdom will be thrown outside, into the darkness, where there will be weeping and gnashing of teeth.

The "subjects of the kingdom" are the Jewish people who, because of unbelief, will be cast from the Messianic Banquet of the age to come. Darkness is another word for Gehenna: "The inheritance of sinners is destruction and darkness" (Ps. Sol. 15:10). The experience of the pain of divine punishment is conveyed by the picture of weeping and gnashing of teeth (cf. Matt. 13:42,50; 22:13; 24:51; 25:30). Weeping and wailing point to the expression of grief, while gnashing of teeth points to rage. (One rabbinic source holds that the tears of regret in Gehenna will be so copious that the flames of torment will be slightly cooled.)[5]

Matthew 10:28; Luke 12:5

> Do not be afraid of those who kill the body but cannot kill the soul. Rather, be afraid of the one who can destroy both soul and body in hell.

The disciples of Jesus must not fear those who can kill only their physical bodies; rather they must fear (reverence) God who, if he so please, can destroy both soul (the real self) and

34

body in Gehenna. The verb *apollumai*, translated "destroy," means "to ruin" through destruction rather than to annihilate; thus Jesus is giving a warning of the consequence of not obeying God.

Matthew 11:23; Luke 10:15

> And you, Capernaum, will you be lifted up to the skies? No you will go down to the depths (= Hades). . . . But I tell you it will be more bearable for Sodom on the day of judgment than for you.

Here Jesus echoes the prophecy of Isaiah upon Babylon (14:13ff.), for Capernaum's impenitence comes from pride, its seeking to make itself like God himself. The town had refused to accept the miracles of Jesus as signs of God's reign, and so it will be humiliated in judgment. The future tense, "it will be more tolerable," points to the resurrection of both good and bad at the judgment. The people of Capernaum will be judged and condemned (going down to the depths, Hades). Heaven and Hades are used here to denote the height of glory and the depth of degredation.

Matthew 24:45-51; Luke 12:42-6

> Who then is the faithful and wise servant, whom the master has put in charge of the servants in his household to give them their food at the proper time? It will be good for that servant whose master finds him doing so when he returns. I tell you the truth, he will put him in charge of all his possessions. But suppose the servant is wicked and says to himself, "My master is staying away a long time," and then begins to beat his fellow servants and to eat and drink with drunkards. The master of that servant will come on a day when he does not expect him and at a hour he is not aware of. He will cut him to pieces and assign him a place with the hypocrites, where there will be weeping and gnashing of teeth.

The opening question calls upon the disciples to choose between two possible types of living—to watch and be ready or
to waste time and be punished. The severity of the punishment for the unfaithful servant is the same as that for the
wicked—separation from the company of the faithful and
confinement to Gehenna. (Compare the similar description
of excommunication from the faithful in the *Manual of Disci-
pline* of the Qumran community: "May he be cut off from the
midst of the sons of light because he swerved from following
God. . . . May he place his lot in the midst of the eternally
cursed" [ii. 16-7].) Thus Jesus again warns his disciples that
the only service God will reward is that which is faithful.

Matthew

There are more references to Gehenna in this gospel than
in any other. One reason for this may be that, being written
within a Jewish milieu for Jewish Christians, it records more
fully Jesus' teaching on rewards and punishments after death
and at the last judgment.

5:22

I tell you that anyone who is angry with his brother will be subject to judgment. Again, anyone who says to his brother, "Raca,"
is answerable to the Sanhedrin. But anyone who says, "You fool,"
will be in danger of the fire of hell.

Here Jesus lists three graded judgments—local court, national
court, and God's court—to warn that evil attitudes expressed
in action or kept in the heart will truly be judged. "You fool"
(Gk. *mōros*) means "You senseless imbecile and apostate."
Jesus warns that hatred of another person can lead to punishment by God in the *fire* of Gehenna (recalling both the original fire-worship of Moloch and the fires of garbage).

13:40-2

> As the weeds are pulled up and burned in the fire, so it will be at the end of the age. The Son of Man will send out his angels, and they will weed out of his kingdom everything that causes sin and all who do evil. They will throw them into the fiery furnace, where there will be weeping and gnashing of teeth.

At the Parousia of the Son of Man, Jesus, there will be a radical cleansing of the Church and a separation of the righteous from the evil—just as there is a separation of wheat from weeds at harvest time. The evil will be condemned to Gehenna, here pictured as a fiery furnace (compare Dan. 3:6). 1 Enoch 10:13 speaks of evil persons being led "to the abyss of fire; in torment and in prison they will be shut up for all eternity." Similar themes occur in other apocalyptic literature.

13:49-50

> This is how it will be at the end of the age. The angels will come and separate the wicked from the righteous, and throw them into the fiery furnace where there will be weeping and gnashing of teeth.

The angels, accompanying and assisting the Son of Man as Judge, gather and separate the good from the bad in preparation for reward or punishment.

16:18

> I tell you that you are Peter, and on this rock I will build my church, and the gates of Hades will not overcome it.

Hades is the realm of the dead and is the Greek word used in the Septuagint to render Sheol, the Hebrew word for the place of the dead. Jesus is here saying that the gates of Hades will not close to imprison in death those who confess that Jesus is Messiah and thus belong to the messianic society. He is promising that life for disciples of the kingdom continues in and through death into the glorious life of the age to come. This being so, then those who are not confessing Jesus as Messiah will be imprisoned by the gates of Hades/Sheol with no hope of life in the kingdom of God.

18:14

> Your Father in heaven is not willing that any of these little ones should be lost.

This statement occurs at the end of the parable of the lost sheep. God does not desire that anyone should permanently lapse from the community of the faithful and thereby perish by exclusion from his presence.

18:23-39. The Parable of the Unmerciful Servant

> (vv. 32-5) Then the master called the servant in. "You wicked servant," he said, "I cancelled all the debt of yours because you begged me to. Shouldn't you have had mercy on your fellow servant as I had on you?" In anger his master turned him over to the jailers until he should pay back all he owed.
> This is how my heavenly Father will treat each of you unless you forgive your brother from your heart.

The unforgiving, says Jesus, will themselves be excluded from God's mercy. As we noted above, the picture of the prison and paying back the last penny point to Gehenna (Matt. 5:25-6). Again Jesus utters a solemn warning.

22:1-14. The Parable of the Wedding Banquet

> (vv. 11-13) When the king came in to see the guests, he noticed a man there who was not wearing wedding clothes. "Friend," he

asked, "how did you get in here without wedding clothes?" The man was speechless. Then the king told the attendants, "Tie him hand and foot, and throw him outside, into the darkness, where there will be weeping and gnashing of teeth."

The wedding garment is probably to be understood as the robe of faithfulness which the righteous wear because they have responded to the gospel and its claims upon them. Without this robe there is no right to be present at the great banquet of the kingdom of God: The alternative to attendance there is the darkness of Gehenna.

23:13-5

Woe to you, teachers of the law and Pharisees, you hypocrites! You shut the kingdom of heaven in men's faces. You yourselves do not enter, nor will you let those enter who are trying to. Woe to you, teachers of the law and Pharisees, you hypocrites! You travel over land and sea to win a single convert, and when he becomes one, you make him twice as much as son of hell as you are.

In Matthew 23 the word "woe" is used seven times: It is a word that is common in the apocalyptic literature and points to the deserving of the wrath of God, in the judgment at the end of the age. Gehenna is introduced to describe the punishment deserved by both the converters and the converted.

23:33

You snakes! You brood of vipers! How will you escape being condemned to hell? Therefore I am sending you prophets and wise men and teachers.

After uttering the woes against the teachers of the law and the party of the Pharisees, Jesus now calls them a brood of vipers, a description which had been used by John the Baptist

(3:7) and Jesus himself (12:34). Their teaching has had a deadly effect upon their disciples. Because of this doctrine and their attitudes, Jesus warns them that they will face condemnation to Gehenna on the day of judgment unless they repent and receive the message of the kingdom of God in the proclamation of prophets and the teaching of wise men.

25:30

> Throw that worthless servant outside, into the darkness, where there will be weeping and gnashing of teeth.

This is the last verse of the Parable of the Talents (cf. Luke 19:12-27) and describes the punishment of the worthless servant who hid his master's money in the ground, making no use whatsoever of it. His punishment is being cast into Gehenna (see 8:12; 13:50; 22:13; 24:51 for similar condemnation).

25:31-46. The Sheep and the Goats

> (vv. 41-46) Then he (Son of Man, King) will say to those on his left, "Depart from me, you who are cursed, into the eternal fire prepared for the devil and his angels . . . Then they will go away to eternal punishment, but the righteous to eternal life.

These words occur at the end of the description of the judgment at the end of the age, executed by Jesus, the Son of Man. As the Shepherd, he divides the people into the sheep (the righteous and faithful) and the goats (the evil and unfaithful). As the right outcome of their genuine faith, the "sheep" served their neighbor what he or she needed; in contrast the "goats" were unaware of the need and so failed to meet it. The condemnation at the judgment is to depart from the King, to be cursed, to enter into eternal fire, there to join the devil, and to endure eternal punishment. Here the language is apocalyptic.

The devil (Satan, Beelzebub) is the chief of a company of rebellious angels, who consistently oppose God and his will for humankind. Gehenna is particularly created for them, where they will be joined by those who think and act like them.[6]

Four times in the New Testament the final state of the wicked is referred to as punishment: here and 2 Thess. 1:9; 2 Pet. 2:9; Heb. 10:29. "Eternal punishment" can mean (1) a process of punishment which lasts for ever or (2) punishment which has eternal results.

Luke

In the material peculiar to this gospel we meet the themes of woe, perishing, and being crushed, together with the separation of the just and unjust in the Parable of the Rich Man and Lazarus.

6:24-26

Woe to you who are rich, for you have already received your comfort.
Woe to you who are well fed now, for you will go hungry.
Woe to you who laugh now, for you will mourn and weep.
Woe to you when all men speak well of you, for that is how they treated the false prophets.

The four woes are the four blessings of verses 20-2 stated conversely. The context leaves little doubt but that they refer to the day of judgment (v. 23 "in that day"), when exclusion from the kingdom of the age to come will be the verdict upon those who do not receive the kingdom now. Thus "how miserable" will be the lot of the unrighteous when faced with divine judgment.

13:3,5

But unless you repent, you too will all perish.

The presence of sin in all people is for Jesus a self-evident fact and in responding to a message about the massacre of Galileans, he calls for repentance in order to avoid the inevitable results of that sin, which are more than physical death. They include the experience of perishing—receiving the results of the adverse judgment of God.

16:19-31. The Parable of the Rich Man and Lazarus, the Poor Man

> (v. 26) Between us and you a great chasm has been fixed, so that those who want to go from here to you cannot, nor can anyone cross over there to us.

These are the words of Abraham as he addressed the rich man (Dives) in the parable. It is possible that in creating this parable Jesus has adapted a folk tale of a rich man and a pious poor man whose fortunes are reversed in the afterlife. He was addressing rich Jews, Sadducees in particular, who failed to use their God-given opportunities provided both by their wealth and their possession of the sacred Torah.

The rich man is a priest who lives luxuriously while professing allegiance to the God and religion of the Torah, which required that he actually care for the poor. He is selfish and indulgent, and he fails to relieve the great need of the beggar whom he sees at the gate of his home. Further, when he contemplates death, he thinks of it as entrance into the shadowy, dark gloom of Sheol/Hades, without any possibility of divine judgment there or bodily resurrection from there.

In the afterlife, to the surprise of the rich man, the position of the two men is reversed. Lazarus is seated next to Abraham at the banquet, with his head on the bosom of the patriarch (v. 22). This is a picture of bliss. In contrast, the rich man, as he had expected, found himself in Hades, the place and sphere of the departed, but it was not the Hades of his previous theology. It was Hades (as some Jewish apocalyptic had taught) divided into Gehenna and Paradise (or places approximating to these), and there was a great chasm between the two halves of Hades.

This parable is merely a story, told for purposes other than establishing a doctrine of the afterlife. This said, it is difficult to avoid concluding that Jesus did himself believe that life after death, both before and after the final judgment, will involve either enjoyment or deprivation of the presence of God and his faithful people.

20:18

Everyone who falls on that stone will be broken in pieces, but he on whom it falls will be crushed.

This ending of the parable of the Tenants in the Vineyard is not found in the Matthean version (21:33ff.). The stone recalls that of Daniel 2:44-45 and here points to the Messiah, who is the pivotal capstone of the new building that is being built in the kingdom of God. To reject him or to be judged by him at the end of the age means to be broken or crushed, as by a large stone. Thus Jesus warns again of the great danger of rejecting the gospel of the kingdom.

John

In this Gospel we do not encounter either the word "Hades" or "Gehenna," but we do meet words and phrases which point to the existence and reality of hell.

3:16

For God so loved the world that he gave his one and only Son, that whoever believes in him shall not perish but have eternal life.

The verb "to perish" (*apollumai*) used here in the intransitive means "to be lost" or "to suffer destruction" (cf. 6:27; 10:28; 11:50). This gospel declares that life is found only in God, who is Father, Son, and Holy Spirit, and that without this Deity a person has no life and is thus lost, perishing and facing destruction. The incarnation and atonement of Christ are the basis for the free gift of life to those who believe; to reject the Son is to reject God's unique gift and to be without the life of the kingdom of God of the age to come.

3:36

> Whoever believes in the Son has eternal life, but whoever rejects the Son will not see life, for God's wrath remains on him.

For the wrath of God to rest and remain upon a person means that he/she is subject to divine punishment and exclusion from the kingdom of God. To reject the Son as the Messiah and the One sent from the Father is to incur the holy wrath of God at the day of judgment.

5:24-9

> Most assuredly, I say to you, he who hears My word and believes in Him who sent me has everlasting life, and will not come into judgment, but has passed from death into life . . . . for the hour is coming in which all who are in the graves will hear His voice and come forth—those who have done good to the resurrection of life, and those who have done evil to the resurrection of condemnation (NKJV).

Those who believe in Jesus as the One sent from the Father will not be condemned in the judgment, for already they have been given the life of the kingdom of God of the age to come. Just before the Final Judgment there will be a resurrection of the dead, but only those who have done evil will be judged,

and it will be a judgement of condemnation to an existence
without the life of God already given to the faithful.

In some apocalyptic literature there is the doctrine that
only the righteous will be raised from Sheol/Hades, but here
and there the doctrine of a general resurrection is found. For
example:

> In those days the earth will return that which has been entrusted
> to it, and Sheol will return that which has been entrusted to it,
> that which it has received, and destruction (Gehenna) will re-
> turn what it owes. And he will choose the righteous and holy
> from among them, for the day has come near that they must be
> saved (1 Enoch 51:1; cf. 4 Ezra 7:32-8).

And there is also the teaching of Daniel 12:2: "Multitudes
who sleep in the dust of earth will awake: some to everlasting
life, others to everlasting contempt." Thus Jesus espouses the
doctrine of a general resurrection followed by the final judgment.

15:6

> If anyone does not remain in me, he is like a branch that is
> thrown away and withers; such branches are picked up, thrown
> into the fire and burned.

This is taken from the image of the vine and branches used by
Jesus to teach that true life and communion with God is in
and through himself as the true vine. In referring to fire and
burning, Jesus is encouraging his hearers to think of Gehenna
as the appropriate place for those who reject life in and
through himself.

17:12

> None has been lost except the one doomed to destruction so that
> Scripture would be fulfilled.

This is part of the priestly prayer of Jesus to the Father and refers to Judas Iscariot. *Apōleia* commonly means eschatological damnation. The same Semitic expression occurs in 2 Thessalonians 2:3 in an apocalypse where it is stated that the Parousia of Christ will not take place until the man of sin and son of perdition be first revealed. It is therefore possible that Jesus saw in Judas such an eschatological character who must appear before the manifestation of the glory of Christ in his death-resurrection-exaltation. In fact the fate of Judas was predicted in Psalm 41:9, and that fate is *apōleia*, casting forth from the presence of God at the last judgment.

Summary

Anyone who goes through the textual evidence cited above cannot but be soberly impressed by the teaching of Jesus. Through such imagery as fire and darkness, prison and abyss, hell is presented both as a state and a place. It is a state in which a person has lost all the blessings that are being heaped upon the righteous; and it is a state wherein a person is cursed, condemned, perishing, under God's wrath, being punished and being destroyed. At the same time it is a place which is distinct from the place of the kingdom of God where the righteous receive their rewards; and it is a place like a prison and an abyss where there is everlasting and unquenchable fire and where the inhabitants weep and gnash their teeth.

Virtually everything that John the Baptist and Jesus said about Gehenna can be paralleled in Jewish literature of the period. However, in that literature there is much greater detail and variety than in the teaching of Jesus. What is distinctive about the words of Jesus is the central and pivotal position he assigned to himself in the future judgment and determination of those whom God will consign to Gehenna. As Messiah and Son he alone says, "Depart from me . . ." (Matt. 25:41).

As the Master, it is he who punishes the unfaithful servant and casts him into "prison" (Luke 12:46). As the Bridegroom, it is he who, when the door is shut, tells the bridesmaids, "I know you not" (Matt. 25:10-12). Therefore we see how Jesus, who came not to destroy the Law and the Prophets but to fill up and fill out their meaning, developed their teaching concerning the End by taking insights and teaching from Jewish apocalyptic literature concerning the destiny of the unfaithful, evil, and wicked.

It is, of course, possible to find ways of setting aside the "harsh" and "terrifying" statements of Jesus concerning hell. One way which is quite common today is to see them merely as a part of a general understanding of eschatology which Jesus shared with many of his contemporaries. This did not constitute divine revelation but was merely a Jewish response to the particular historical situations the people encountered during the Greek and Roman rule. Therefore what Jesus had to say about hell can be discounted and set aside.

The position being advocated in this book is that Jesus did make statements about hell, usually in the form of warnings to avoid it. These statements are as much divine revelation as his teaching on other topics. However, this said, it is recognized that the interpretation of the imagery used by Jesus is not an easy task. Here we offer some further thoughts on Gehenna and fire.[7]

1. *Gehenna.* Examining the sayings of Jesus concerning Gehenna we find that they fall into two categories. First of all, *warnings* addressed to his disciples concerning hindrances, stumbling-blocks, and conditions governing personal destiny (Matt. 5:22,29,30; 10:28; 18:9; Mark 9:43,45,47; Luke 12:5). Secondly, *condemnation* of Jewish religious leaders (Matt. 23:15,33).

In these sayings the word "if" frequently occurs. Jesus did not say, "You are going to Gehenna"; rather, he said, "If you do this or fail to do that you will go to Gehenna." Then, also, in these sayings are references to the whole body and to parts of it (eyes, hand, and feet); this may suggest that Jesus actually had the real valley of Hinnom in mind when he spoke of Gehenna. Thus we recognize that we are dealing with figurative language and that Jesus is using Gehenna in much the same way as did other Jewish teachers of his day.

With reference to the condemnation of the Pharisees and their converts, we may observe that though the judgment appears harsh, it is realistic. First, as guides of the people they were leading them astray, and in Old Testament terms it is "Woe unto the pastors" who do not feed or wrongly feed the flock. The catalog of sins in 23:3-32 contains the most serious of offences against God. Secondly, the condemnation uttered by Jesus is hardly as severe as some of the condemnations of the faithless and apostate in Jewish apocalyptic sources.

2. *Fire.* We have noted the use of fire by Jesus (e.g., Matt. 5:22; 18:8-9; 25:41; Mark 9:43), but only brief comment has been made on the origin and significance of this image. Four observations may be made concerning the background to the use of this word in apocalypticism and by Jesus in particular. First, as we have noted there is the fact of the ever-burning fires of the garbage in the valley of Hinnom and the background there of fire-worship. Second, there is the lake of torment and the oven of Gehenna to which reference is made in 2 Esdras 7:36. Since the fire of a volcano was known to come from within the bowels of the earth, then it was easy to think of Gehenna in terms of an oven of fire and also in terms of molten lava (a lake of torment). Third, ordeal by fire was a common punishment in the ancient world, and the Jewish apocalypses give examples of the persecution of faithful Jews in this manner. So the fire of punishment was a natural image of the afterlife (see e.g. 4 Maccabees 12:11-12). Fourthly, and of most importance, is the connexion between God and fire. He appeared to Moses in a flame of fire (Exodus 3:2), and he caused brimstone and fire to fall upon Sodom and Gomorrah

(Genesis 19:24). His ministers are a flame of fire (Psalm 104:4), and he consumes his enemies with his fiery flame (Sirach 45:19).

In conclusion we may say that while Gehenna, fire, darkness, and perdition are images, they point to a spiritual reality more terrible than the means used to symbolize and highlight it. Thus the Church has seen in the words of Jesus the seeds of the doctrine of the everlasting punishment of those who reject the gospel of God declared by Jesus. We shall examine the doctrine of hell as it has been set forth by the Church over the centuries in Part 2. In the next chapters we shall examine what the apostles taught concerning heaven and hell.

Notes

[1] In the Septuagint *apollumi* usually means destruction in the sense of earthly death and extinction. However, it is also linked with Sheol/Hades in Prov. 15:11; 27:20; cf. Job 26:6; 28:22. This same balance of meaning is reflected in the Synoptic Gospels. Often it means to kill (Matt. 2:13; 12:14; 21:41; Mark 9:22; Luke 17:27, etc.) or to destroy (Matt. 5:29; Mark 1:24, etc.). Sometimes it points to more than physical death and suggests the idea of punishment after death, as in Matt. 10:39; Mark 8:35; Luke 9:24, and Luke 19:10, 13:3,5, and Matt. 18:14. This theological meaning is more prominent in John's Gospel and the Letters of Paul. See further *The New International Dictionary of New Testament Theology*, ed. Colin Brown, Grand Rapids, MI, 1975, vol. 1, 462ff.

[2] See further R. A. Stewart, *Rabbinic Theology*, Edinburgh, 1961, 157. Gehenna is the grecised form of the Hebrew Ge-Hinnom. The valley of Ge-Hinnom lies fairly close to the Old City of Jerusalem and is visible from the summit of the Mount of Olives. It was reputed to have three entrances, one in the wilderness, one in the sea, and one in Jerusalem.

[3] David Hill, *The Gospel of Matthew*, Grand Rapids, MI, 1981, 92.

[4] See further Stewart, *Theology*, 157ff.

⁵ The Midrash Rabbah on the Book of Exodus, vii. 4. Cited by Stewart, 159.

⁶ See further Appendix 1, "Encounter with Satan."

⁷ See further William Strawson, *Jesus and the Future Life*, London, 1959, chap. 7.

·CHAPTER·
3

Jesus, Exalted into Heaven

The Gospels were written after the exaltation of Jesus and the sending of the Spirit in his name by the Father to the disciples. These four documents reflect the conviction that Jesus has been raised from the dead and declared to be the Messiah and Lord at his exaltation to the Father's right hand in heaven. However, this conviction and interpretative principle does not prevent the writers from presenting accurately the ministry, teaching, and passion of Jesus as the center of their proclamation of the Good News of the arrival of God's kingdom. Therefore we have used the Gospels to discover what Jesus actually taught about heaven and hell.

Before we proceed in later chapters to review the teaching of the rest of the New Testament on these topics, it is necessary to assess the importance of the ascension of Jesus into heaven, for, as we shall see, it is assumed by the apostolic writers that the entry of Jesus into heaven caused an objective change in the system of conditions and relationships within heaven. In fact, in terms of a Christian understanding of heaven we may say that heaven was created by the exaltation there of the Son of Man. To appreciate this claim we shall look briefly at the way heaven is portrayed in Scripture prior to the arrival there of the resurrected Jesus. We shall also notice how the Ascension is described and interpreted in the New Testament.

Heaven before the Ascension[1]

In both the Old Testament and New Testament *šamayim* and *ouranos*, the words for heaven(s), are used in one of two ways. They may describe what we would call the skies or the firmament as well as what we would call God's unique "place" and "abode." In Genesis 1 we read that God created the heavens or skies, while in Deuteronomy 26:15 God is asked to "look down from thy holy habitation, from heaven, and bless thy people" (RSV). There was of course a connection between the two in Israelite thinking, for God's holy habitation was usually thought of as above and beyond the physical universe. In the intertestamental literature there is the assumption of a series of heavens, only the first of which is visible to the human eye, and above which is God's own holy habitation.

Heaven is the place where God is specially present, in that he works there more richly and revealingly, bestowing his presence by a more obvious and visible providence than on earth, by a more abundant grace, causing those present to be transparent to his glory and love. Such a way of explaining heaven leaves open the important assertion that God is also present in and through his creation. Heaven, as God's place, is also the place of his hosts, the company of created beings we normally call angels. To think of them as winged is false: such a belief is based on a confusion of them with seraphim and a wrong interpretation of Daniel 9:21 (basing too much on "swift flight"). The form of an angel is beautiful and impressive, evoking a sense of the divine as the patriarchs knew (Gen. 18; 32:22ff.) or a sense of dread as the woman of Judges 13:6 knew. In their reflection of the divine glory the angels differ from the demons, and in that they are not made of flesh and blood and exist without sex or mortality, they differ from human beings. While the angels do enter space and time as the messengers of God, their permanent abode is in heaven where God is surrounded by them as they form his heavenly council. Not only Isaiah in his great vision (Isaiah 6) but also Micaiah "saw the Lord, sitting on his throne, and all the host of heaven standing beside him at his right hand and on his left" (1 Kings 22:19). Because of the particular way in which they were created by God, the worshipping and obedient angels do not need a mediator between themselves and God; their task is to be the servants and messengers of the Lord.

Medieval theological students discussed almost endlessly where the righteous dead of the old covenant went. Had they gone directly to heaven to join the angels in the worship of God, or had they gone to a place specially created by God as the place of waiting (but waiting in peace and joy) until the Messiah actually opened the kingdom of heaven to faithful believers? There is little information in the Old Testament to provide an answer to these questions. Certainly the hope of the resurrection of the dead appears in the apocalyptic passages of Isaiah (26:19) and Daniel (12:2). But such a hope is of a historical future in God's presence. However, here and there we encounter passages in the Psalms (e.g., 23; 48) which may express a confidence that at death the righteous believer enters God's holy habitation. Psalm 16:11 seems to express this confidence explicitly: "In your presence there is fullness of joy, at your right hand *are* pleasures for evermore" (NKJV).

In the intertestamental literature there is the assumption that the *psychē* of a good man is in the hands of God, in contrast to that of the bad man which is either in Hades or Gehenna. Then from the appearance of Moses and Elijah on the Mount of Transfiguration, as well as from the Parable of Dives and Lazarus as told in the New Testament, there is further confirmation that the righteous of the old covenant are safe with God. But all this information does not answer the question whether the righteous dead have joined the heavenly host and are actually in heaven or whether they are in a place God has specially created for them until the Messiah's work is done? The idea of *limbus patrum* (the limbo of the fathers) arose in medieval theology because it was held that heaven was closed to human beings from the time of Adam's fall into sin until the Messiah became the way into heaven for faithful believers. This limbo was a place of happiness and was distinct from purgatory which was a place of purging enroute for limbo/heaven; after the ascension on Jesus, limbo disappeared for, it was held, he led the saints of the old covenant into heaven as their Savior and Mediator. Thus we must be careful of dogmatism with respect to the whereabouts of the righteous of the old covenant; we can certainly say that they were safe in the hands of God but we cannot be sure that they entered heaven until the One for whom they looked, the Messiah of Israel, led them in his name and by his merits into that place where the angels for ever worship the Lord.

The Ascension of Jesus into Heaven[2]

Two accounts are provided by Luke of the final departure of Jesus, the Ascension. First, is the short account in Luke 24:50-2:

> When Jesus had led them out to the vicinity of Bethany, he lifted up his hands and blessed them. While he was blessing them, he left them and was taken up into heaven. Then they worshiped him and returned to Jerusalem with great joy.

It will be recalled that Luke begins with a reference to the righteous priest, Zechariah, who is unable to give God's blessing to the congregation of (old) Israel (1:21-2). But it closes with a portrait of Jesus, the resurrected high priest of the new and true Israel, blessing his people. Zechariah went into the Temple in Jerusalem with a prayer for the redemption of Israel; the disciples of Jesus went into the same temple about thirty-three years later in joy and thanksgiving for the actual redemption of Israel achieved by Jesus. All we learn of the departure of Jesus is that he was taken up by the power of God into heaven, God's holy habitation.

Second, is the longer account in Acts 1:3-11, from which we learn that Jesus had been appearing intermittently to the disciples over a period of forty days. At this last appearance Jesus told them:

> You will receive power when the Holy Spirit comes on you; and you will be my witnesses in Jerusalem, and in all Judea and Samaria, and to the end of the earth.

After he had said this

> he was taken up before their very eyes and a cloud hid him from their sight. They were looking intently up into the sky as he was going when suddenly to men dressed in white stood before them. "Men of Galilee," they said, "why do you stand here looking into the sky? This same Jesus who has been taken from you into heaven will come back in the same way you have seen him go into heaven."

It is this account, and this only, that refers to the period of "forty days" during which Jesus made himself present and visible to his disciples. Also it is this account which describes the ascent of Jesus not merely into the sky but into the cloud. The latter is not any cloud but the special cloud called the Shekinah, which descended upon the Tabernacle in the wilderness (Exod. 13:21; 40:34; 1 Kings 8:10-11). With it came the presence and glory of the Lord; and so to enter it was to enter the holy of holies, the immediate presence of God himself.

Jesus had to be taken up into heaven before the Father could send the Holy Spirit to indwell, empower, and guide the disciples, for the Spirit is the Paraclete of Jesus. The account of how the Spirit actually came and what an impact his coming had is found in Acts 2. Further, we learn from Acts 1 that Jesus will return to earth in power and glory in the Shekinah, just as he had left. So this passage asserts the relationship between the Ascension and heaven, between the Ascension and the sending of the Spirit, and between the Ascension and the Parousia.

What Luke describes as occurring on the fortieth day is not to be understood as the first and actual ascension of Jesus into heaven. Rather what he presents is a visible and symbolic portrayal of what already had happened on Easter morning when God raised Jesus from the dead and exalted him to heaven. No one witnessed the resurrection/ascension/exaltation on Easter morning except the angels. What the disciples saw was the empty tomb and the risen Lord Jesus, who came to them from heaven, accomodating himself to their sight and understanding. Jesus continued to come to them as the exalted, heavenly Lord for a period of forty days and then on that last day, what had truly happened to him was symbolically presented through his departure into the Shekinah. His going up into the cloud portrayed that he was now permanently in heaven as the Messiah.

Theology of the Ascension/Exaltation

1. In his ascension *Jesus conquered hostile powers;* he overcame the host of Satan in his triumphal procession from Hades (real death) to heaven (God's holy habitation).[3] This interpretation is based on three texts: 1 Peter 3:18-20, Colossians 2:15, and Ephesians 4:8. The first speaking of Christ states that, "being put to death in the flesh but made alive in the spirit; in which he went and preached to the spirits in prison, who formerly did not obey, when God's patience waited in the days of Noah" (RSV). This has been understood in various ways—e.g., of Jesus preaching in the realm of the dead (Hades) in order to convert souls, or his proclaiming to

the saints in limbo that he is the Christ in the period between Good Friday and Easter Sunday. It is better to interpret this text as describing the activity of the risen and ascending Jesus on Easter morning. Transformed by the Spirit, Jesus proclaims to the fallen, evil angels in the lower regions of the air their condemnation by God, and his exaltation to the Father in heaven as the victorious Messiah.

Colossians 2:15 speaks of Christ who "disarmed the principalities and powers and made a public example of them, triumphing over them" (RSV). Here Christ is presented as stripping off himself the evil spiritual forces which had attacked him and clung to him in his passion and death and then leading them in a triumphal procession as the defeated enemy. Ephesians 4:8 cites Psalm 68:18 to declare both the victory of Christ over the host of evil angels and his sending, as the exalted Christ, spiritual gifts to his people on earth.

2. Jesus has been exalted to sit at the right hand of the Father and is to be given the name of Lord.[4] In the first Christian sermon, the apostle Peter declared that God has raised Jesus to life and exalted him to his right hand (Acts 2:33-4). Then he proceeded to quote from Psalm 110:1. "The LORD says to my Lord: 'Sit at my right hand until I make your enemies a footstool for your feet.' " The picture of the Messiah, a descendent of king David according to his human nature and sitting at God's right hand, had been used by Jesus himself in discussions with the Pharisees (Mark 12:36). The "right hand" was the position of the greatest honor, the place of perfect happiness and the exercise of authority and power; it was also the place of rest after the enemies had been overcome.

Thus Jesus sitting at the Father's right hand is a way of saying that he shares the glory, authority, and holiness of the Father. Another way of expressing a similar thought is to say that "Jesus is Lord." In the moving poem of Philippians 2:5-11, Paul depicts Jesus as being exalted to heaven and given the name of "Lord," which is God's own name. While the

picture of sitting at God's right hand evokes the idea of resting after overcoming enemies, that of standing there (as
Stephen saw in his vision of Jesus, Acts 7:55-6) evokes the
further ideas of Jesus vindicating his faithful witness (martyrs)
and of his preparing to return to earth as King and Judge.

3. While exalted as Lord, *Jesus intercedes for the people* of
the new covenant. In Romans 8:34 Paul describes Jesus both
at the right hand of the Father and "also interceding for us."
The One to whom all authority has been given is himself interceding. He is speaking to the Father, not on behalf of himself but on behalf of others. This is not a picture of the
incarnate Son on bended knees beseeching a reluctant heavenly Father to grant favors to those whom he does not wish to
bless. It is rather a picture of the crowned Prince, who enjoys
the total favor of the King, requesting that his friends will always be the recipients of the King's favor and grace.

Because of the claims of the New Testament that Jesus, the
Word made flesh, shares the authority, power, and rule of
the Father and acts as Lord of the Church and Mediator of the
new covenant, we have to say that heaven was dramatically
changed by the arrival and coronation of Jesus as Messiah and
Lord. His presence and exalted position brought a transformation of the system of conditions in which the society and
company of heaven enjoy the presence of the Lord and worship and serve him. For now there is in heaven, in the very life
of God himself, a glorified humanity belonging to the eternal
Son and a humanity of the same essence as shared by the
whole human race. Now created human beings can be drawn
nearer to God than can the holy angels, for the former possess
the same human nature as the Son possesses, and so in and
through him they can draw near to God. This communion
with God could not occur before the exaltation of Jesus as the
incarnate Son; thus theologians have spoken of heaven being
either created or transformed by the resurrection and ascension of Jesus, the Christ.

Notes

[1] See further Ulrich Simon, *Heaven in the Christian Tradition*, London, 1958, chaps. 1-4.

[2] See P. Toon, *The Ascension of Our Lord*, Nashville, 1984, for greater detail.

[3] For greater detail see W. J. Dalton, *Christ's Proclamation to the Spirits: A Study of 1 Peter 3:18–4:6*, Rome, 1965.

[4] For the use of Psalm 110 see D. M. Hay, *Glory at the Right Hand: Psalm 110 in Early Christianity*, New York, 1973.

·CHAPTER·
4

The Heavenly Commonwealth

Having already looked at the teaching of Jesus on heaven, we proceed now to look at the teachings of Paul, the writer of the letter to the Hebrews, Peter, and John as we find them in the New Testament. We approach these teachings knowing that these writers assumed that God had raised Jesus from the dead and exalted him into heaven. For them heaven is truly heaven because their Lord is there, from where he sends to them his Spirit.

Paul on heaven

The continuity between the teaching of Jesus and his apostle to the Gentiles, St. Paul, is not perhaps immediately obvious; however, it becomes so after careful reading of the Pauline Letters and reflection upon their contents. Jesus taught in expectation of his vindication and exaltation, while Paul taught in the light of the resurrection and ascension of Jesus; but there is a golden thread which unites their message.

In the first place there is a correspondence or identity between "the arrival of *the* time" (Mark 1:15) and "*the* time fully come" (Gal. 4:4; cf. Eph. 1:10). In and with Christ, the time of this evil world has come to an end, and the time of the kingdom of God, the new creation, the great salvation, and the new age has dawned. Then, in the second place, the saying of Jesus to his disciples in Matthew 13:11,16,17 finds a real echo in Paul's teaching about the revelation of the mystery in Romans 16:25,26 (cf. Col. 1:26; Eph. 1:9,10; 3:4,5; 1 Cor. 2:7; 2 Tim. 1:9,10). To the inner circle of disciples, Jesus said, "Blessed are your eyes because they see and your ears because they hear the knowledge of the secrets of the kingdom of heaven." To the community of believers Paul declared that the hidden counsel of God concerning his redeeming and saving activity was now revealed in word and in deed in Christ and by his Spirit. Therefore, though Paul hardly uses the expression "kingdom of God" and though his vocabulary is often rather different from that of Jesus, there is an underlying unity in what they proclaim, teach, and confess.

Paul told the church in Corinth that "now is the time of God's favor, now is the day of salvation" (2 Cor. 6:2). He referred not merely to any day as the day of opportunity but to the decisive and long expected coming of God to bring redemption and salvation which had arrived with the ministry of the Messiah. Thus he had earlier stated that "if anyone is in Christ, he is a new creation; the old has gone, the new has come!" (2 Cor. 5:17) He meant that to become a Christian by being united with Christ, a person entered into a new order, a new creation. This is obvious from the neuter plural—the "old things" referring to the unredeemed world and evil age with its sin and sadness and the "new things" pointing to the re-creation of all things in and through Christ.

The apostle taught that as a part of this new order the believing community enjoyed the gift and presence of the Holy Spirit, by whom it was united to its Lord, who was exalted in heaven, the same Lord whom they expected to return so that this evil age would end and the fulness of salvation would come.[1]

We have a limited task in this chapter. Since Paul's theology is so rich we cannot look at all its hints and intimations of heaven and heavenly life. We shall therefore examine those important texts in which the apostle actually specifically speaks of heaven. We shall find as we look at these texts that Paul did not write about heaven as God's place in a general way but in a specific way: For him heaven was truly heaven because Jesus, the Lord, the Last Adam, and the Head of the Church was there sharing the glory of the Father and sending the Holy Spirit to the faithful on earth.

Thus as we look at specific texts from the Epistles we must keep in mind this Christological approach to heaven. Paul knew well the teaching of the Hebrew Bible on heaven as God's holy habitation, there worshipped and adored by the angels. He also was aware of the developments in the intertestamental literature and in rabbinical teaching. It was, however, through the revelation from Christ which he received as an apostle that he created a specifically Christocentric doctrine of heaven.[2]

Galatians 4:26

> The Jerusalem that is above is free, and she is our mother

Paul wrote the letter to the churches of Galatia in order to combat certain heresies. One of these emphasized the city of Jerusalem as the center of Judaism as a corollary to the emphasis upon the need for Christians to keep the basic rules of Judaism. Thus Paul was opposing Judaizers and proclaiming salvation and freedom in Christ when he wrote his letter. He presented an allegory of two mothers, Hagar and Sarah, in order to contrast two covenants and two cities. The earthly Jerusalem, which Paul knew well, was the "mother" of legalism and the symbol of the covenant God made with Moses at Sinai (Exodus 19); the heavenly Jerusalem (the heavenly realm where Christ is the exalted Lord) is the mother of the believing faithful (the true children of Sarah), who are members of the new covenant, inaugurated by Christ's sacrificial blood, shed at Calvary.

The picture of Jerusalem, or Zion, as mother is found in the Old Testament. Psalm 87:5 states that "of Zion it will be said, 'This one and that one were born in her and the Most High will establish her'" (Cf. also Isa. 50:1; Jer. 50:12; Hos. 4:5). As the quotation of Isaiah 54:1 in Galatians 4:27 shows, Paul quite deliberately took what had been said of the earthly Jerusalem and claimed it for the heavenly one. That is he freely interpreted the prophecies of Isaiah 40-66 which spoke of Jerusalem in God's purposes in the light of the death and exaltation of Jesus, the Christ.

The concept of a rebuilt and transformed Jerusalem was common in rabbinic teaching, while the concept of a new Jerusalem descending from heaven to earth to replace the old city was common in apocalyptic texts.[3] Paul differed because he taught that there was no further place for the old Jerusalem in God's salvific purpose and that the heavenly Jerusalem actually really now exists as the center of God's forward moving history of salvation. It exists because Christ is really and truly in heaven as the One who by his death and resurrection has set his people free from the bondage of the covenant of Sinai and of legalism. Thus Christian believers are not enslaved to the law and not under obligations to Jerusalem in Judea; they are truly free, for "it is for freedom that Christ has set us free" (5:1). Jesus Christ is the genuinely free man, and thus the heavenly realm, the mother of the faithful, is the center of true freedom, the freedom that characterizes the new age.

1 Corinthians 15:47-9

> The first man was of the dust of the earth, the second man from heaven. As was the earthly man, so are those who are of the earth; and as is the man from heaven, so also are those who are of heaven. And just as we have borne the likeness of the earthly man, so shall we bear the likeness of the man from heaven.

Here Paul compares Adam, the man created from the dust of the earth and the representative of the earthly order (Genesis 2-3) with Jesus, the Man raised from the dead and exalted to the Father's right hand and Representative of the heavenly order. Paul writes that the first man is of the earth and earthly while the second man is *of* (rather than "from") heaven and thus heavenly. Paul is not saying that Jesus was pre-existent and came from heaven (as translations may suggest) but that, as the resurrected Christ, the life-giving Spirit, he is now in heaven and that his existence in his transformed but real humanity is heavenly. (This interpretation works on the assumption that *ex ouranou* and not *anthropos ex ouranou* is the predicate in v. 47b.)

Believers are said to be heavenly not because they have come from heaven or are going to heaven but because they are "in Christ," the Man of heaven, and share his resurrection life. This heavenliness will be fully expressed in the resurrection body in the life of the age to come. In this present age believers bear the image of Christ and are being transformed according to that image as they live within the confines of their mortal bodies in hope. The participation in heavenliness is, therefore, not the restoration of what has been lost through the Fall, but the receiving of a new quality of existence. In fact, that which is given in Jesus to those who believe is that which God always has planned for his people; heavenly existence is the goal of humanity and in Jesus it is both reached and freely given.

2 Corinthians 5:1-4

Now we know that if the earthly tent we live in is destroyed, we have a building from God, an eternal house in heaven, not built by human hands. Meanwhile we groan, longing to be clothed with our heavenly dwelling, because when we are clothed, we will not be found naked. For while we are in this tent, we groan and are burdened, because we do not wish to be unclothed but to be clothed with our heavenly dwelling, so that what is mortal may be swallowed up by life.

Before writing these words Paul had been defending his apostleship by showing how his tribulation, trials, and physical weakness have become evidences of his calling as an apostle. Of himself and close colleagues he wrote: "Though outwardly we are wasting away, yet inwardly we are being renewed day by day. For our light and momentary troubles are achieving for us an eternal glory that far outweighs them all. So we fix our eyes not on what is seen, but on what is unseen. For what is seen is temporary, but what is unseen is eternal" (4:16-18). That which is not seen and is of everlasting permanence is the fact of the resurrection of Jesus and his existence and rule in the heavenly realm.

The picture of the earthly tent-dwelling (= mortal body and "earthen vessel") highlights the temporary nature of life on earth in this evil age; in comparison the heavenly tent-dwelling (= the resurrection body) is permanent and indestructible since it comes directly from God himself. At death the earthly tent-dwelling disintegrates, but if the believer is alive at the Parousia then it will be transformed by the power of God into the heavenly tent-dwelling. This raises the question as whether the believer who dies before the Parousia (1) becomes a naked spirit waiting until the Parousia to be clothed with his heavenly tent-dwelling or (2) receives immediately after death his heavenly tent-dwelling. The present tense of v. 1 "we have" *(echomen)* points to a certainty, but does it necessarily point to an immediate succession between the earthly and heavenly forms? It could be a futuristic present used by Paul because he was so confident of the future possession of the resurrection body at the Parousia. To support this it can be maintained that the general drift of Paul's teaching in 1 Corinthians 15 is to link the gaining of resurrection bodies with the Parousia of Christ. Opinion is divided be-

tween those who believe that Paul taught in the "intermediate state" believers exist as "naked spirits" or as clothed in
their heavenly tent-dwelling.[4]

2 Corinthians 12:2-4

> I know a man in Christ who fourteen years ago was caught up to
> the third heaven. Whether it was in the body or out of the body I
> do not know—God knows. And I know that this man—whether
> in the body or apart from the body I do not know, but God
> knows—was caught up to Paradise. He heard inexpressible
> things, things that man is not permitted to tell.

What Paul describes in vv. 1-10 was not a unique vision but
an outstanding example of his visionary experiences, which
came to him after the first "heavenly vision" (Acts 26:19; cf.
9:1-22; 22:3-16; 26:9-18) which made him into both a Christian and an apostle, as he saw the heavenly Lord Jesus.

Fourteen years before writing to Corinth (i.e., between AD
41-44) Paul was caught up to the third heaven (v. 2), a variant
designation of Paradise (v. 4). Already we have noted that Paradise refers to the abode of the righteous who have passed
through death; here Paul describes how he felt the experience
so intensely that he was not sure what was the mode of the
rapture. The idea of a sealed revelation occurs in the Old Testament (see Isa. 8:16; Dan. 12:4) and more commonly in
apocalyptic literature, and thus Paul's sealed lips represent a
hallowed tradition within Judaism.[5]

Paul's vision is to be understood as an experience of deeper
fellowship and intimacy with the resurrected and exalted
Lord Jesus, who is at the center of Paradise. Even so, he was
not removed from or relieved of sharing in the suffering of
Christ. His thorn in the flesh—be it physical pain or the continuing opposition of his enemies—was not removed so that
he could experience heavenly power in earthly weakness.

Philippians 1:23-4

> I desire to depart and be with Christ, which is better by far; but it is more necessary for you that I remain in the body.

As Paul faces the possibility that he will not survive his imprisonment, he expressed his dilemma. As a believer who is "in Christ" and who already has had a revelation of the heavenly realm, Paul longs to be with Christ in that sphere. He believes that death is the door into the presence of Christ; yet as an apostle who cares deeply for the Gospel and the churches, he feels that he ought to continue to pursue his apostolic labors on earth.

Philippians 3:20-21

> But our commonwealth is in heaven, and from it we await a Savior, the Lord Jesus Christ, who will change our lowly body to be like his glorious body, by the power which enables him even to subject all things to himself. (RSV)

The RSV has been used because of its translation of *politeuma* as "commonwealth." This is much to be preferred to the "citizenship" of NEB, NKJV, and NIV or "homeland" of JB. The meaning Paul intended to convey was that our state and constitutive government is in heaven, for that is where Christ reigns as Lord.[6] Thus faithful believers living on earth in mortal bodies are truly citizens of the heavenly realm where Christ is King. And they are assured that at the Parousia this heavenly *politeuma* will become the central and guiding reality of the kingdom of God of the age to come, in which they will live in their new, immortal, and glorious bodies.

Colossians 3:1-4

> Since, then, you have been raised with Christ, set your hearts on things above, where Christ is seated at the right hand of God.

Set your minds on things above, not on earthly things. For you
died, and your life is now hidden with Christ in God. When
Christ, who is your life, appears then you also will appear with
him in glory.

The resurrection of Jesus took him from the realm of the dead
to the heavenly realm where he is supreme. Paul made use of
Psalm 110:1 (cf. 1 Cor. 15:25 and Rom. 8:35) to convey the
idea of Jesus, as the victorious Messiah, sitting at the right
hand of the Father at rest and in glory. Believers in Christ
have been raised (aorist tense) with Christ. Because, therefore, they truly belong to the heavenly realm, they are to set
their hearts on Christ who is above, while they are yet on
earth. In fact their baptism symbolized that in Christ they
have died to sin and have been raised to the heavenly realm
above all evil and sin. So their day-to-day life is to reflect what
their baptism signified. Then, at the Parousia, when Christ is
revealed in all his glory, the reality of the genuinely heavenly
life of believers will also be manifested.

Ephesians

This letter, which we assume is Pauline, is permeated with
belief in the reality of the heavenly realm, where Christ sits at
the Father's right hand. The "Berakah" or Blessing of 1:3-14
celebrates what God has accomplished in exalting Jesus and
creating the Church. "Praise be to the God and Father of our
Lord Jesus Christ, who has blessed us *in the heavenly realms*
with every spiritual blessing in Christ" (v. 3). Here we encounter the formula *en tois epouraniois* which is also found at
1:20; 2:6; 3:10; 6:12. It appears not to mean simply "heaven"
as "God's Place," since at 3:10 and 6:12 the presence of fallen
angels is presumed to be there. Thus, against the background
of Old Testament and Jewish apocalyptic literature teaching
that the upper limits of the firmament/heavens were inti-
mately linked to heaven as the invisible, created reality of

God's holy habitation, it is best to take this expression as having a double thrust. It refers both to that place where Christ is enthroned, surrounded by the adoring angels and to that sphere between God's "place" and the firmament where the fallen angels gather to seek to thwart the purposes of God for the redemption of the world. Believers united to Christ rejoice that their Lord and Savior is in the "upper" heavenly realm, "above" the fallen angels.

In 1:15-23 Paul prays that his readers will appreciate the true nature of God's raising of Jesus to his right hand as the place of victory, power, rest, and honor, and appreciate his becoming the Head "over everything for the Church, which is his body, the fullness of him who fills everything in every way" (v. 23). The raising of Jesus has placed him permanently above all the cosmic hierarchy of angels and archangels. Paul cites Psalm 8:6 (which recalls Gen. 1:26-8) to show that, as the Last Adam, Christ has been given universal dominion over heaven and earth, angels and humans, and that he directs them to their appointed goal in God's will. God has given this supremacy to the heavenly Man, Jesus, to be used on behalf of the Church, which itself has a special role in God's plan for the universe. In fact, the Church is the body of Christ in that he fills this *ekklēsia* of God with his Spirit, grace, power, and gifts.

What God has done for Christ he has also done for those who are "in Christ Jesus." We saw in Colossians 3:1 how Christians are to seek the things above in heaven, because of their union with Christ who is above. In Ephesians 2:4-6 Paul strengthens this call by writing that "God, because of his great love for us . . . made us alive with Christ and raised us up with Christ and seated us with him in the heavenly realms in Christ Jesus." This heavenly reality is of course hidden to human eyes and will become obvious only at the Parousia. Nevertheless, it is created by grace alone and provides a great incentive to holy and single-minded living for God in this evil age.

Paul insists that the incorporation into Christ is not for in-dividualistic purposes, for as he wrote:

> You are no longer foreigners and aliens, but fellow citizens with God's people [lit. "holy ones" = angels] and members of God's household, built up on the foundation of the apostles and prophets, with Christ Jesus himself as the chief cornerstone [or top stone]. In him the whole building is joined together and rises to become a holy temple in the Lord. And in him you too are being built together to become a dwelling in which God lives by his Spirit (2:19-22).

The Gentiles have become part of God's Temple, the Church, the new sphere in which God makes himself known and his presence felt. In short, the Church is the heavenly temple with its "foundation stones" being the apostles and prophets and its crowning or top stone in the heavenly realm being Christ himself. So the whole temple is dominated by Christ, whose Spirit indwells the whole.

This Church is to incorporate and reflect the breakdown of the barriers between Jew and Gentile; the resulting unity in and through Christ by the Holy Spirit becomes a pledge of the certain overcoming of all cosmological dualism and Sa-tanic opposition by the achievement of perfect harmony in the age to come. "God's intent was that now, through the Church, the manifold wisdom of God should be made known to the rulers and authorities in the heavenly realms, accord-ing to his eternal purpose which he accomplished in Christ Jesus our Lord" (3:9-10). In this present period of time wherein there is an overlap of the ages, the evil angels still have power to oppose God's will and thwart his purpose, but the unity and harmony achieved by the work of Christ will ultimately apply to the whole cosmos and all evil will finally be defeated.

As the ascended and exalted Lord, Jesus has given and con-tinues to give spiritual gifts to his Church on earth as it seeks to maintain the unity of the Spirit (4:3).

To each one of us grace has been given as Christ apportioned it. This is why it says: "When he ascended on high, he led captives in his train and gave gifts to men." (What does "he ascended" mean except that he also descended . . . ? He who descended is the very one who ascended higher than all the heavens in order to fill the whole universe.) (4:7-10).

In citing Psalm 68:18 Paul modified the Septuagint text, involving a change of person from the second to the third person. In its original setting the quotation celebrated the Lord's deliverance of his people as he is pictured ascending Mount Zion, driving before him the captives of battle from whom he receives tribute. For Paul the ascent of Zion becomes Christ's ascent "through the heavens" into the true heaven of God; it involves triumphing over evil angels (Eph. 1:21; Col. 2:15) *en route*, in order to become the cosmic Lord with an universal rule and in order that he would constantly fill all things with his authority and power. He also ascended to give spiritual grace and send gifts to his Church. But what is the descent? It has been explained in terms of a descent into Hades between Good Friday and Easter Day, or the descent of the pre-existent Christ from heaven in his incarnation, or of the descent of the exalted Christ in the Spirit as his Paraclete at Pentecost. The latter seems the best interpretation in this context where Paul emphasizes that Christ gives spiritual gifts to his Church.

As recipients of gifts, faithful believers, members of the one Church, are involved in a battle against Satan and all his hosts. However, they fight as those who, in Christ, have won the decisive battle even though the war has not ended. They are in Christ in the heavenly realm and so fight from this position and perspective.

Finally be strong in the Lord and in his mighty power. Put on the full armor of God so that you can take your stand against the devil's schemes. For our struggle is not against flesh and blood, but against the rulers, against the authorities, against the powers of this dark world and against the spiritual forces of evil in the heavenly realms (6:10-12).

This struggle continues until the Parousia when all evil and demonic powers will be finally vanquished. Meanwhile, human relationships are given new significance and purpose when they are seen in the light of the believer's union with Christ in the heavenly realm (5:21ff. and 6:9).

In summary we may say that for Paul heaven is not only where Christ, the true image of God, now is, but it is also where he will be after his Parousia. United to the Father, in Christ and by the Spirit, the believing community belongs to that sphere where Christ, its Savior, Lord, and Mediator is. And he is at the right hand of the Father in the glory of heaven, where the angels for ever worship and serve him. For Christians the true commonwealth is then the heavenly realm which by reason of its nature and the One in it is to believers as the mother of the faithful. Not only is hope laid up for the faithful in heaven (Col. 1:5), but as those who are led by the indwelling Spirit and who are, in Christ, already exalted to heaven, they are to set their hearts and minds upon this heavenly realm and live their lives in the light of this special relationship.

While "looking up" they are also to "look forward," waiting for the appearance from heaven of the Lord Jesus, knowing that in him they are rescued from the coming wrath (1 Thess. 1:10). They long for the Parousia, since the return of the Lord Jesus will mean the end of this evil age, the establishment of the kingdom of God in its fullness, and the enjoyment of eternal life, which is the "end" of sanctification (Rom. 6:22). For this new age, new creation, and fullness of salvation, they will receive immortal, resurrection bodies of glory. In anticipation they "are being transformed (now) into

73

his likeness, with ever-increasing glory, which comes from the Lord, who is the Spirit" (2 Cor. 3:18).

Meanwhile they know, as Paul did, that if they die before the Parousia, they will be with the Lord Jesus—whether as naked spirits or with resurrection bodies is not clear. The important point is that they are to be convinced that "neither death nor life, neither angels nor demons, neither the present nor the future . . . will be able to separate them from the love of God that is in Christ Jesus their Lord" (Rom. 8:38-9). Further, as the great hymn of love puts it: "Now we see but a poor reflection; then we shall see face to face. Now I know in part; then I shall know fully, even as I am fully known" (1 Cor. 13:12).

Hebrews[7]

In this fascinating letter, there is a contrast between Christianity and Judaism: Christianity is acclaimed as superior in every way because of the very excellence of the incarnate Son and High Priest, Jesus the Messiah. Thus heaven through, with, and by this Jesus as Priest-King is central to the new order which Christianity proclaims. We shall examine the teaching on heaven under five themes.

1. *The Sabbath-Rest*

There remains a Sabbath-rest for the people of God; for anyone who enters God's rest also rests from his own work, just as God did from his. Let us, therefore, make every effort to enter that rest, so that no-one will fall by following their example of disobedience (4:8-10).

When believers have completed their service and work on this earth and in this age they will enter into the Sabbath-Rest, that is, participation in God's own rest. In six days, states Genesis 1, God created the universe and on the seventh day he rested. That is, he contemplated what he had made and rejoiced in it (like a painter enjoying his painting after finishing it). Also the Lord Jesus, after offering himself as a sacrifice for sin on Good Friday, rested in the tomb on Holy Saturday, the Great Sabbath, and looking upon the travail of his soul, he was satisfied with the new creation.

The rest of God is not that kind of rest which is inertia, boredom, and stagnation; rather it is perfect and unruffled life. God, who is changeless, is active and actual infinite fullness to which nothing can be added or subtracted. As Father, Son, and Holy Spirit—One God—he is perfectly active and rested in the unity and interchange of love. In Christ the people of God enter in God's rest now, but the fullness of the rest is to come. Heaven means participation in God's rest.

2. The Throne

> Let us fix our eyes on Jesus, the author and perfector of our faith, who for the joy set before him endured the cross, scorning its shame, and sat down at the right hand of the throne of God (12:2).

Earlier Jesus had been described as our high priest "who sat down at the right hand of the throne of the Majesty on heaven" (8:1). Thus here is the image of the throne of God and of Christ, based on Psalm 110 and often used in the apostolic teaching.

To this joint-throne Christians are to go: "Let us approach the throne of grace with confidence, so that we may receive mercy and find grace to help us in time of need" (4:16). Thus heaven is where God the Father shares his throne with his incarnate Son, the Priest-King. The heavenly throne is a mercy seat, the antitype of the earthly mercy seat of the Temple (see 9:5 and cf. Leviticus 16 and Exodus 25). This image forcibly proclaims that propitiation for sin has been made and that there is now forgiveness and mercy with God through

Jesus. At the heart of heaven where the Father and Son reign (1:8, "Your throne is for ever") there is mercy, for Jesus the High Priest, who has been tempted in every way as we are, is there!

3. *The Sanctuary (Tabernacle, Holy Place)*

> For Christ did not enter a man-made sanctuary that was only a copy of the true one; he entered heaven itself, now to appear for us in God's presence (9:24).

Jesus, the High Priest, enthroned with God, discharges his ministry not in an earthly sanctuary but in the true and real sanctuary, the heavenly dwelling-place of God. There he "serves in the sanctuary, the true tabernacle set up by the Lord, not by man" (8:2).

The idea of a sanctuary not made with human hands is found both in the teaching of Jesus (Mark 14:58; John 2:19ff.) and of Stephen and Paul (Acts 7:48; 17:24). This new sanctuary obviously includes the temple of the Holy Spirit—the people of God understood as the "house of God" (note 3:6, "we are his house" and see also Isa. 66:1ff., quoted by Stephen). Therefore, the sanctuary is that spiritual realm that originates where Christ is with the Father and that comes to us in and through the person and work of the Holy Spirit. It is the heavenly realm which, though not a part of this world and age, may be encountered and entered in the Holy Spirit from within this world and age. Yet at all times it is wholly dependent on the ministry of the exalted Lord Jesus as Priest-King with the Father. In the new age of the fullness of the kingdom of God which is to come, the sanctuary will be wholly expressed in the perfection of the communion of the saints one with another and all with God in Christ. Thus this new sanctuary, invisible but very real, is the true sanctuary of which the Jewish Tabernacle and Temple were but material copies.

4. The City of God

All these people were still living by faith when they died. They did not receive the things promised; they only saw them and welcomed them from a distance. And they admitted that they were aliens and strangers on earth. People who say such things show that they are looking for a country of their own. If they had been thinking of the country they had left, they would have had opportunity to return. Instead, they were longing for a better country—a heavenly one. Therefore God is not ashamed to be called their God for he has prepared a city for them (11:13-16).

The patriarchs lived their lives convinced that God would fulfill the promises he had made to them. And in death they continued to look forward for their realization—"By faith Isaac blessed Jacob and Esau in regard to their *future*" (v. 20). Neither Mesopotamia nor Canaan was their true home, for they desired and looked for another place where God would be more real to them. They longed for the "city of God."

Why is the image of the city so important both here and (as we shall see) in Revelation 21:10-11,23-26? We need to remember that the ancient city was understood as a holy place, at the center of which was a holy shrine, where it was believed heaven and earth met. The city walls enclosed an area of safety and order and offered protection from all foes, human and spiritual. Inside, the people were to live in peace, harmony, and brotherhood under the just rule of the king, who was seen as anointed and as set in power by the deity. Thus his palace adjoined the central shrine. For us today the city is perhaps the symbol of decay, decadence, and deprivation. But for people in the ancient near East it was a powerful symbol of fellowship with and care by the living God. Jerusalem became such a symbol for the Israelites. Here God dwelt in the Temple, and the king, anointed by God, lived in his palace next to the Temple, ruling his people in righteousness. At least this was the ideal (Psalms 46,48), and when it was not realized, the image became the source of promise and hope (Isaiah 60, 66; cf. Revelation 21).

Heaven is like the ideal of the ancient city—a place of harmony, brotherhood, peace, and joy, where there is perfect fellowship with the Lord God.

> But you have come to Mount Zion, to the heavenly Jerusalem, the city of the living God. You have come to thousands upon thousands of angels in joyful assembly, to the church of the first-born, whose names are written in heaven. You have come to God, the judge of all men, to the spirits of righteous men made perfect, to Jesus the mediator of a new covenant, and to the sprinkled blood that speaks a better word than the blood of Abel (12:22-4).

Thus heaven includes angels, the faithful of the Old Covenant (spirits of righteous men), all Christian believers (church of the first-born) and at its center, Jesus himself, whose sacrificial blood brings cleansing, forgiveness, and peace (not a cry for vindication as with Abel).

5. *The kingdom*

> He has promised, "Once more I will shake not only earth but also the heavens." The words "once more" indicate the removing of what can be shaken—that is, created things—so that what cannot be shaken may remain. Therefore, since we are receiving a kingdom that cannot be shaken, let us be thankful, and so worship God acceptably with reverence and awe, for our God is a consuming fire (12:26-9).

At the end of the present age there will be a cosmic convulsion. But the heavenly realm wherein Christ is the Priest-King cannot be and will not be shaken by the final judging and purging activity of God. It is a kingdom that is everlasting and to this kingdom belong all those who are faithful believers in Christ Jesus. What this kingdom really and truly means will be wholly apparent only after the cosmic convulsions and the birth of the new age.

Heaven in this letter is not only that which is "above" where Christ is and "in the future" when the kingdom of God comes in fulness, but also the heavenly realm into which, by the Spirit, the faithful are admitted while still in this world and age.

1 and 2 Peter[8]

For Peter heaven is where Jesus Christ now is: Following his resurrection Christ "has gone into heaven and is at God's right hand—with angels, authorities and powers in submission to him" (1 Pet. 3:22). From there the Holy Spirit descends to earth (1 Pet. 1:12) to continue the work of Christ in and among the faithful. These, because they have an imperishable inheritance reserved in heaven (1 Pet. 1:4) and are called to eternal glory (1 Pet. 5:10), know that they are aliens and strangers in this world and age (1 Pet. 2:11). In fact they belong to God as his chosen people, royal priesthood, and holy nation (1 Pet. 2:9) so that they can begin now their everlasting service of declaring his praises.

As pilgrims in this world, the believing faithful know that this world must come to an end in order that the new universe can be created as its replacement: "In keeping with his promise, we are looking forward to a new heaven and new earth, the home of righteousness" (2 Pet. 3:13). John also expressed this hope (Revelation 21), which we shall note below.

John on heaven[9]

In the Introduction we briefly discussed apocalyptic literature, noting that its most productive period was from 200 BC to AD 100. The last book of the Bible, the Apocalypse of

John, not only belongs to this literary genre but is also the source of the name "apocalyptic." Though sharing common features with the Jewish books (for example, an open heaven and visions) the book we call Revelation is decidedly Christian in both content and orientation. We do not know the identity of the author who had these visions either around AD 68 or 95. All we can say is that his name was John, that he was imprisoned for his faith, and that he had good knowledge of the situation of the seven churches of Asia which he addressed (chaps. 2-3).

Unlike his contemporary Jewish apocalypticists, John did not put his message in the name of a person of the past. Rather he described himself as "your brother and companion in suffering" and one who had prophetic words to share. Therefore his authority is that of one who has been moved by the Holy Spirit and who has received a message from the risen and exalted Lord Jesus. Thus he could end the book with these words:

> I warn everyone who hears the words of the prophecy of this book: if anyone adds anything to them, God will add to him the plagues described in this book. And if anyone takes words away from this book of prophecy, God will take away from his his share in the tree of life and in the holy city, which are described in this book (22:18-9).

The three opening chapters and concluding section (22:8-21) stand apart from the apocalypse proper and form a framework in which it has been set. So 4:1 begins, "After this I looked, and there before me was a door standing open in heaven. And the voice I heard speaking to me like a trumpet said, 'Come up here and I will show you what must take place after this.'" Up to this point John had reported the words of the risen Christ who had appeared to him (1:9ff.), but from this point onward he speaks of what he has seen in the opened heaven. The vision of God's holy habitation and throne in 4:1-11 is an Old Testament picture of heaven, recalling Isaiah 6 and

Ezekiel 1. It is heaven *before* the exaltation of Jesus, so that the vision of heaven *with Jesus* (5:1-14) is contrasted.

In the vision of chapter 4, John saw the Lord seated upon his throne as the sovereign reigning King, who is Creator of the universe. The twenty-four elders (probably related to the twenty-four priestly and levitical orders), symbolize the adoration and worship of heaven addressed to God, Creator and King; the four cherubim, as sentinels by the throne, also unceasingly offer worship: "Holy, holy, holy is the Lord God Almighty, who was, and is, and is to come" (4:8). On earth, where John lived, few acknowledged that the Lord is the Creator and King, but John is privileged to listen to the choirs of heaven celebrating the sovereignty of God. The reference to what looked like a sea of glass, clear as crystal, in front of and behind the throne, serves to emphasize that there is always a distinction between God and creatures, even those who are in his immediate vicinity (cf. Ezek. 1:22).

In the vision of chapter 5 the attention is turned from God as Creator to God as Redeemer, and the Lord Jesus Christ as the Lamb of God is introduced. John sees in the right hand of God, the Creator, a scroll with seven seals: It records the divine will for the inauguration of events which lead up to the new age and creation. Only when the seals of this scroll are broken can the process begin. But who can break these seals? John weeps because no one is sufficiently worthy to accomplish this task. "Then one of the elders said to me, 'Do not weep! See, the Lion of the tribe of Judah, the Root of David, has triumphed. He is able to open the scroll and its seven seals'" (5:5). Jesus, described as the Lion of Judah (Gen. 49:9) and Root of David (Isa. 11:1,10), is alone worthy, for he is the Lamb, "looking as if it had been slain" (i.e., with a slit throat), who was offered on Mount Calvary; further, he possesses royal power (seven horns) and is omniscient (seven eyes).

Then John saw what may be called a coronation ceremony, where the ascended Jesus is crowned King of kings and Lord of lords, as he is given all authority in heaven and on earth. "The Lamb came and took the scroll from the right hand of him who sat on the throne. And when he had taken it, the four living creatures and the twenty-four elders fell down before the Lamb" (vv. 7-8). While the coronation and the acclamation of the hosts of heaven (elders, cherubim, and myriads of angels, vv. 8-11) lies in the past, since Jesus is crowned, the acclamation of "every creature on heaven and on earth and under the earth and on the sea" must wait till the end of the age. Then all shall sing, "To him who sits on the throne and to the Lamb be praise and honor and glory and power, forever and ever!"

It has been said that chapters 4–5 are the fulcrum of the whole book. In relation to what has gone before they provide an understanding of the Person who wrote to the churches, and in relation to what shall be, they serve the purpose of initiating the series of judgments which end with the descent of the city of God from heaven to earth. We must pass over these frightening judgments in order to learn of heaven from the last part of the Apocalypse.

Before he was granted the vision of a new heaven and a new earth, John saw the vision of the overthrow of the enemies of Christ (19:11-12), the creation of the millennial kingdom (20:1-8), the doom of Satan (20:7-10) and the final judgment before the great white throne. Though theologians have never been able to agree on the interpretation of the Millennium, in the context of both Old Testament prophecies (Isa. 11:1-11; Dan. 12:2-3, etc.) and apocalyptic vision (4 Ezra 7:27ff.; Syriac Baruch 29ff.), John's vision of a two-fold expectation of the arrival of the kingdom of God makes sense, but it has few, if any, parallels in contemporary Jewish literature. In the first stage, the Millennium, God's purpose *within* history is openly vindicated within that history and during the *present* age. The martyrs especially are vindicated (11:11) as truly worthy to be priests and kings (5:10). In fact the vision of the Millennium reflects the conviction that the present creation is a sphere to reflect the will of God, for when Satan is restrained it is not so corrupt as to be beyond hope.

The climax of the Apocalypse comes in 21:1-7.

> Then I saw a new heaven and a new earth, for the first heaven and the first earth had passed away, and there was no longer any sea. I saw the Holy City, the new Jerusalem, coming down out of heaven from God, prepared as a bride beautifully dressed for her husband. And I heard a loud voice from the throne saying, "Now the dwelling of God is with men, and he will live with them. They will be his people and God himself will be with them and be their God. He will wipe away every tear from their eyes. There will be no more death or mourning or crying or pain, for the old order of things has passed away."
>
> He who was seated on the throne said, "I am making everything new!" Then he said, "Write this down, for these words are trustworthy and true."
>
> He said to me: "It is done. I am the Alpha and Omega, the Beginning and the End. To him who is thirsty I will give to drink without cost from the water of life. He who overcomes will inherit all this, and I will be his God and he will be my son."

Within Jewish apocalyptic and rabbinic teaching there is also the hope of the new cosmos, either in terms of a totally cleansed earth, impregnated with the glory of God, or of a totally new universe. John's vision is of the latter since there is the absence of any sea. The important feature of the new cosmos is the holy city, which is the only part of the new heavens and new earth that John is allowed to see. This new and heavenly Jerusalem is not the earthly, rebuilt city in the Holy Land, but a direct creation of God, designed to fulfill abundantly for redeemed and sanctified humanity the role which the prophets saw for the earthly Jerusalem in relation to Israel and the Gentile nations (Isa. 2:1-5; 49:14ff.; 54:1ff.).

As John saw the holy city descending he heard God declare

that he would permanently dwell with his new creation so that there would be perfect fellowship and union between himself and themselves. Redeemed humankind will actually see God and live! And everything that made the old order and age imperfect and unsatisfying will be absent from the new order and age (Isa. 25:8; 35:10; 51:11). In verses 5-8 God himself speaks to insist that all things will certainly be new, for he himself will make them new. The ancient promise of Isa. 55:1, "Come all you who are thirsty, come to the waters," will be abundantly fulfilled as will also the promise made to king David, "I will be his father and he shall be my son" (2 Sam 7:14). The new creation will be fellowship par excellence and perfect harmony between God and man.

It is reasonable to assume that the section 21:9–22:5 is an extended comment or exposition of the words in 21:1-4 concerning the descent of the holy city. We shall look at two parts of this section. First, 21:22-27:

> I did not see a temple in the city, because the Lord God Almighty and the Lamb are its temple. The city does not need the sun or the moon to shine in it, for the glory of God gives it light, and the Lamb is its lamp. The nations will walk by its light and the kings of the earth will bring their splendor into it. On no day will its gates ever be shut, for there will be no night there. The glory and honor of the nations will be brought into it. Nothing impure will ever enter it, nor will anyone who does what is shameful or deceitful, but only those whose names are written in the Lamb's book of life.

The earthly temple had been the symbol of the presence of God in an imperfect world and a reminder of two distinctions essential to Israelite and Jewish faith—that between the holy and the common and that between the clean and unclean. In the new Jerusalem no such symbol is needed, for the sphere of the holy and the clean have expanded to cover everything in the new creation. The Lamb of God, the exalted Messiah, retains his office as Mediator in the new order and age; in and through him there is both constant access and total communion with God. And the glorious splendor and brilliance of God and the Lamb is such that the luminaries of the old creation are redundant. The Lamb is the true light of the new world. Further, the nations and peoples who have been deceived by Satan and his servants in the old order will come into the city to bring their worship, service, and tribute to the Lord God and to the Lamb. Yet they will come as the redeemed people of God, the elect, whose names are written in the book of life.

The second part is 22:1-5:

> Then the angel showed me the river of the water of life, as clear as crystal, flowing from the throne of God and of the Lamb, down the middle of the great street of the city. On each side of the river stood the tree of life, bearing twelve crops of fruit, yielding its fruit every month. And the leaves of the tree are for the healing of the nations. No longer will there be any curse. The throne of God and of the Lamb will be in the city and his servants will serve him. They will see his face and his name will be on their foreheads. There will be no more night. They will not need the light of a lamp or the light of the sun, for the Lord God will give them light. And they will reign for ever and ever.

The river of the water of life significantly begins at the throne of God and the Lamb (recalling the words of Jesus in John 7:37-39) and flows through the city between avenues of trees which line the banks (cf. Gen. 2:9 and Ezek. 47:7ff.). The fruit of these trees symbolizes fullness of life in God's presence. This fullness is necessarily linked to the fact that redeemed humanity sees the face of God, the highest of all human possibilities and privileges. This attaining wholly by grace of the *visio dei* is the climax of salvation and becomes the constant and continuing experience of the elect of the new creation, as will also be participation in the sovereignty of God and the Lamb.

The imagery of Revelation 21-22 is heavily dependent

upon the Old Testament portrayals of the Garden of Eden and the City of God. However, its main themes, which complement those we have seen in the teaching of Jesus and the apostle Paul, are clear. In the new order, which already exists in God's holy habitation, Christ is central for he is the Mediator between God and mankind. There will be intimate fellowship between God and redeemed humanity with the absence of all that gives pain and sorrow and with the abundant presence of all that gives joy and life. Members of the new creation will actually see God and thus will be truly blessed.

Notes

[1] Of all the books on Pauline theology, I have found Herman Ridderbos, *Paul: An Outline of His Theology*, Grand Rapids, MI, 1975, the most helpful.

For Paul in the context of Judaism, W. D. Davies, *Paul and Rabbinic Judaism*, Philadelphia, 1980[4], is still very helpful even if E. P. Sanders, *Paul and Palestinian Judaism*, Philadelphia, 1977, has made us see that the situation is very complex.

I have used a variety of commentaries on Paul's Letters: e.g., C. E. B. Cranfield on Romans, C. K. Barrett on 1 Corinthians, H. D. Betz on Galatians, Markus Barth on Ephesians, F. W. Beare on Philippians, Eduard Schweizer on Colossians.

[2] I am deeply indebted to Andrew T. Lincoln's book, *Paradise Now and Not Yet: Studies in the Role of the Heavenly Dimension in Paul's Thought, with Special Attention to Eschatology*, for the choice of texts and many illuminating ideas (Cambridge University Press, Monograph Series for the Society of New Testament Studies, No. 43, 1981).

[3] See, e.g., Jub. 4:26; Ps. Sol. 11:8; Test. Levi 10:5; 1 Enoch 90:28f. See also the Qumran literature—1QM 12,13ff.; 4Qp Isa.[a] 1,7,11.

[4] See further Murray J. Harris, *Raised Immortal*, Grand Rapids, MI, 1984, chap. 4.

[5] For texts and discussion see Lincoln, *Paradise*, 82. Rowland, *The Open Heaven*, 380ff has a good discussion of Paul's vision.

[6] This is Lincoln's suggestion. See his discussion of *politeuma*, 97ff.

[7] I have found the commentaries of F. F. Bruce (Grand Rapids, MI, 1964) and Hugh Montefiore (New York, 1964) very helpful.

[8] I have found the commentary of J. N. D. Kelly on *I & II Peter* (New York, 1964) helpful and Richard Bauckham on 2 Peter (in *Jude & II Peter*, Waco, Texas, 1983) most illuminating.

[9] I have particularly used George R. Beasley-Murray's commentary (Grand Rapids, MI, 1981); Robert H. Mounce's study (Grand Rapids, 1977) was also helpful.

·CHAPTER·
5

The Lake of Fire

In this chapter it is our task to survey what is presented in the New Testament, apart from the Gospels, concerning hell. Apart from noticing the use of the specific word, "hell," we shall also look at texts which speak of death, destruction, perdition, punishment, and fire.

Pauline teaching

Romans 2:5-9

> Because of your stubbornness and your unrepentant heart, you are storing up wrath against yourself for the day of God's wrath, when his righteous judgment will be revealed. God "will give to each person according to what he has done." To those who by persistence in doing good seek glory, honor and immortality, he will give eternal life. But for those who are self-seeking and who reject the truth and follow evil, there will be wrath and anger. There will be trouble and distress for every human being who does evil . . .

Paul is addressing a Jew who is a Jew only in name, not in faith and faithfulness. For our purposes they key words are "storing up wrath," "the day of God's wrath," his "righteous judgment will be revealed," "wrath and anger," and "trouble and distress."[1] The day of wrath is the day when God will judge men's hearts and secrets through Jesus Christ (2:16). On that day God's righteous judgment will be fully exhibited and executed. "Wrath and anger/indignation" will be the rewards of disobedience for the ungodly; these terms describe the retribution of the ungodly in terms of God's displeasure: "Trouble and distress" describe their punishment in terms of their experience.

6:23

> For the wages of sin is death, but the gift of God is eternal life in Christ Jesus our Lord.

The figure here is probably a military one, referring to the soldier's daily provision money; this is contrasted with the free gift, or bounty, which was distributed to the army on the accession to the throne of a new emperor. Sin pays her soldiers with death; God's bounty provides them with eternal life in Jesus Christ. Death is contrasted with eternal life and obviously means more than mere physical death (cf. 6:16), fearful even as that is. As a minimum, "death" means to be deprived of participation in the life of the kingdom of God of the age to come[2] (cf. further references to death in 7:5,10,13; 8:6,13.)

1 Corinthians 1:18

> For the message of the cross is foolishness to those who are perishing, but to us who are being saved it is the power of God.

Paul preached a Savior who had been crucified and had risen from the dead. This message made nonsense to those who are perishing (*apollumenois*). This verb in the present participle implies that they will not merely perish in the future but they are definitely on the way to perdition now (cf. 2 Cor. 4:3). Perdition refers not only to the extinction of physical existence but also to the deprivation of the favor of God in the afterlife. It is of interest to note that in the Qumram texts the ungodly are called "men of perdition" (IQS) and "sons of perdition" (CD; cf. 2 Thess. 2:10).

6:9

> Do you know that the wicked will not inherit the kingdom of God? Do not be deceived: Neither the sexually immoral nor idolators . . . will inherit the kingdom of God.

The kingdom of God is thought of here as future, coming into full reality after the Parousia of Christ. The theme of inheritance[3] is present in both Old Testament and New Testament pointing to the fulfillment of God's promises and the hopes of the righteous. From this future glory the wicked and unrighteous will be excluded.

2 Corinthians 2:14-16

> Thanks be to God, who always leads us in triumphal procession in Christ and through us spreads everywhere the fragrance of the knowledge of him. For we are to God the aroma of Christ among those who are being saved and those who are perishing. To the one we are the smell of death; to the other, the fragrance of life.

Paul pictures the apostles as joyful participants in the triumphal procession of Christ, their commander. Perhaps also he sees perfumes sprinkled along the triumphal way as signs of celebration. Certainly he used a rabbinical description of the Torah ("a fragrance of knowledge") in order to describe Christ as the embodiment of knowledge and truth. And the apostles as proclaimers of the gospel concerning this Christ share the fragrance and become the aroma of Christ.

However, the perfumes which increased the joys of the triumphant also brought misery to those being led to execution. So the fragrance of the knowledge of God in the gospel on the one hand tells of life and leads to life and on the other is deadly in nature and effect. To reject the Christ of the gospel is to join those who are on their way to perdition (cf. 1 Cor. 1:18 and 2 Cor. 4:3-4.)

7:10

> Godly sorrow brings repentance that leads to salvation and leaves no regret, but worldly sorrow brings death.

While genuine sorrow before God, who is gracious, leads to a right relationship with him and into his salvation, a false or worldly sorrow, which is directed towards self-pity, leads to a wrong relationship with him and entails death. As we noted above with reference to Romans 6:23, death is more than the end of physical life: It is the opposite of salvation.

Galatians 1:8-9

> Even is we or an angel from heaven should preach a gospel other than the one we preached to you, let him be eternally condemned! As we have already said, so now I say again: If anybody is preaching to you a gospel other than what you accepted, let him be eternally condemned!

This shows how seriously Paul viewed the truth of the gospel entrusted to him. "Let him be" is a solemn affirmation of what certainly shall be: "eternally condemned" translates "anathema," a cognate of *anathēma*, meaning something yielded up to the wrath of God and thus surrendered to the curse of God.[4]

5:19-21

> The acts of the sinful nature are obvious . . . I warn you, as I did

before, that those who live like this will not inherit the kingdom of God.

This is much the same as 1 Cor. 6:9. Living in sin in the present prevents entry into the kingdom of God now and thus an inheritance in the kingdom of God of the age to come. The future tense "will not inherit" conveys the idea of certainty of this lot (see also Col. 3:6 and Eph. 5:5-6 for similar teaching).

6:7-8

> Do not be deceived: God cannot be mocked. A man reaps what he sows. The one who sows to please his sinful nature, from the nature will reap destruction; the one who sows to please the Spirit, from the Spirit will reap eternal life.

The whole of life is a period of sowing, and the harvesting is God's judgment at the end of the age. Destruction or corruption (*phthera*) is not the cessation of human existence in or after death: it is the positive existence of grief and woe both in this life and the life to come after death.[5] Such is the harvest of the seed of self-interest. The seed of "faith working through love" has the harvest of eternal life in the kingdom of God of the age to come.

Philippians 1:27-28

> Whether I come and see you or only hear about you in my absence, I will know that you stand firm in one spirit, contending as one man for the faith of the gospel without being frightened in any way by those who oppose you. This is a sign to them that they will be destroyed, but that you will be saved—and that by God.

The enmity against the church and the endurance of the believing community under great difficulties are a sign of two facts: the perdition of the opponents and the salvation of the believers. "Will be destroyed" is contrasted with "will be saved" and is obviously a reference to the results of the judgment of God at the end of the age. The Greek word is *apōleia*, and it is again used in 3:18-19.

1 Thessalonians 5:1-3

> Now, brothers, about times and dates, we do not need to write to you, for you know very well that the day of the Lord will come like a thief in the night. While people are saying, "Peace and safety," destruction will come on them suddenly, as labor pains on a pregnant woman, and they will not escape.

Already in 1:10 Paul has connected the Parousia of Christ with the revelation and execution of the wrath of God. Here he writes again of the Second Coming of the Lord Jesus as Judge. For those who are unprepared to receive him it will be a time of calamity, for destruction will be their lot as the judgment. "Destruction" translates *olethros*, which points to a state of utter and hopeless ruin (cf. 2 Thess. 1:9).[6] This point is underlined by the comment that "they will not escape."

2 Thessalonians 1:6-10

> God is just: he will pay back trouble to those who trouble you, and give relief to you who are troubled and to us as well. This will happen when the Lord Jesus is revealed from heaven in blazing fire with his powerful angels. He will punish those who do not know God and do not obey the gospel of our Lord Jesus. They will be punished with everlasting destruction and shut out from the presence of the Lord and from the majesty of his power on the day when he comes to be glorified in his holy people and to be marvelled at among all those who have believed.

The advent from heaven of the Lord Jesus with flaming fire as his robe and accompanied by mighty angels recalls not only the teaching of Jesus in Matthew 25:31 but a theme within Jewish apocalyptic. Because he comes as Judge his activity will include giving vengeance (cf. Deut. 32:35), that is, imposing the just penalty upon those who do not know (= are not in spiritual communion with) God the Father and who do not believe and obey his Gospel. These people will be punished by being given what they deserve and merit as those who have rejected God's self-revelation in Jesus. They will face everlasting destruction (*olethros*), complete ruin in the age to come ("Everlasting destruction" is found also in the same form in the Greek in 4 Maccabees 10:15, where it is the lot of the wicked tyrant and is contrasted with the blessed death of the Jewish martyr.). Everlasting destruction is further explained in terms of being shut out from and excluded from the presence (literally "face") of God and from his great glory.

Summary of Paul's teaching. Paul does not use the word "Gehenna" in these epistles. However, he does speak of God's wrath and anger being displayed in the judgment against the wicked; further, he refers to the results of that judgment in terms of death (in contrast to eternal life and salvation), of destruction (in contrast to salvation), of perdition (in contrast to salvation), of punishment (in contrast to reward), and of thereby not inheriting the kingdom of God and not seeing the face of God in the age to come. And he insists that the lot of the wicked is decided by Jesus Christ as the Judge, acting in behalf of the Father. It is possible to find in the intertestamental literature all the ideas that Paul employs concerning the fate of the wicked. What is unique to Paul is his insistence that Jesus of Nazareth in his Parousia decides what this fate shall be.

Nowhere in his epistles does Paul specifically teach that there will be a resurrection of the ungodly. He is more than clear that there will be a resurrection of the believers, but concerning the resurrection of the rest of humankind he has nothing to say. Yet we may presume that he did teach a general resurrection since, according to Luke, he told Felix that "there will be a resurrection of both the righteous and the wicked" (Acts 24:16).

Hebrews

2:2-3

> For if the message spoken by angels was binding, and every viola-
> tion and disobedience received its just punishment, how shall we
> escape if we ignore such a great salvation?

The message mediated by angels was the Law of Moses in which every commandment has an appropriate penalty pre-scribed for its infringment. The Gospel of salvation was brought to earth by the eternal Son of God: To ignore or to reject him is to be exposed to sanctions far greater than those prescribed in the Torah. Implied in the question, "how shall we escape . . .," is the answer, "there is no escape" from pun-ishment at the "eternal judgment" (part of the "elementary teaching" mentioned in 6:1-2; cf. 9:27).

10:26-31

> If we deliberately keep on sinning after we have received the
> knowledge of the truth, no sacrifice for sins is left, but only a
> fearful expectation of judgment and of raging fire that will con-
> sume the enemies of God. Anyone who rejected the law of
> Moses dies without mercy on the testimony of two or three wit-
> nesses. How much more severely do you think a man deserves to
> be punished who has trampled the Son of God under foot, who
> has treated as an unholy thing the blood of the covenant that
> sanctified him, and who has insulted the Spirit of grace? For we
> know him who said, "It is mine to avenge; I will repay," and
> again, "The Lord will judge his people." It is a dreadful thing to
> fall into the hands of the living God.

The deliberate and persistent sinning here described is the Christian equivalent of the Old Testament description of sinning "with a high hand" and "defiantly" (Numb. 15:30), for which no pardon was provided in the law of atonement. The author must be referring to definite and calculated apostasy and renunciation of Christ and Christianity. And the penalty for it is severe. The expectation of raging fire at the divine judgment is a recalling of Isaiah 26:11: "Let the fire reserved for your enemies consume them."

To reject the Law of Moses means incurring the penalties of the law. To reject or spurn the Son of God and what he has achieved and stands for must and will incur greater penalty than that of the Mosaic Law. The Song of Moses (Deuteronomy 32) contained warnings from the Lord (35-36) that he is Judge and will execute judgment and impose punishment on those who defiantly forsake his covenant and grace—and these warnings are cited here. Let it not be forgotten that the God and Father of our Lord Jesus Christ is the *living* God, and for those who reject his Beloved Son it is and will be a fearful thing to fall into *his* hands at the judgment. "Our God is a consuming fire" (12:29, citing Deut. 4:24).

James

4:12

> There is only one Lawgiver and Judge, the one who is able to save and destroy.

James writes of the last judgment when all must face the Author of the Torah who is the Judge of the world. He alone can save and he alone can send to destruction (*apollumi*).

5:20

> Whoever turns a sinner away from his error will save him from death and cover a multitude of sins.

Death is more than physical dying: It is also the penalty of sin and final exclusion from the society of the kingdom of God of the age to come. Thus anyone who causes a person who is on the way to such a fate to turn around and seek God enables that person to receive forgiveness and have his sins blotted out.

2 Peter

2:4-9

> For if God did not spare angels when they sinned, but sent them to hell, putting them into gloomy dungeons to be held for judgment; if he did not spare the ancient world when he brought the flood on its ungodly people but protected Noah, a preacher of righteousness, and seven others; if he condemned the cities of Sodom and Gomorrah by burning them to ashes, and made an example of what is going to happen to the ungodly; and if he rescued Lot, a righteous man, who was distressed by the filthy lives of lawless men . . . If this is so then the Lord knows how to rescue godly men from trials and to hold the unrighteous for the day of judgment, while continuing their punishment.

Peter provides three examples of the impartial judgment of God: upon the pride and rebellion of fallen angels, the apathy and disobedience of the men of Noah's day, and the excessive sensuality of the men of Sodom (cf. Jude 5-7). Later, he shows that God's just judgment upon the present world will certainly also occur (3:8-10). It is possible that Peter's account of the fallen angels (Gen. 6:1-4; cf. Rev. 12:7) is influenced by knowledge of 1 Enoch, where there is teaching concerning the punishment of evil angels (e.g., 10:4-6; 18:11-21:10). "Sent them to hell" is a single word in the Greek and means "consigned them to Tartarus," the place in Greek mythology of the punishment of the departed spirits of the very wicked. In this Gehenna within Hades they wait for the final judgment at the Parousia of Christ.[7]

Peter believed that the God who has delivered, delivers,

and will deliver the righteous is also the God who has judged, judges, and will judge the unrighteous. Thus the fate of the wicked will be similar to if not identical with that of the fallen angels; and this will be worse than the latter's present fate. The last part of verse 9 can be understood in two different ways: (1) as referring to the present torment and future judgment of deceased sinners who are in Tartarus; and (2) as indicating that they are being kept now (but not in Tartarus) for a judgment to be made in the future (as the marginal reading of the NIV allows). Each interpretation includes final judgment, but only one definitely indicates that there is punishment before the final judgment.

3:7

By the same word (of God) the present heavens and earth are reserved for fire, being kept for the day of judgment and destruction of ungodly men.

Judgment by fire is one of the great Old Testament pictures of the Day of the Lord (Isa. 13:9ff.; 29:6; 30:30; 64:1,2; 66:15-16; Dan. 7:9-11) and is also common in the intertestamental literature (1 Enoch 10:3; Sib. Orac. 3:71ff.). It is apocalyptic imagery, and so it is difficult to determine whether the transformation of the whole universe through fire or the fiery judgment of sinful men at the judgment is intended. God, as a consuming fire (Deut. 4:24; Mal. 4:1) will on the last day consume what is wicked and refine what is good. This will occur (see 3:8-13) before the arrival of "a new heaven and a new earth, the home of righteousness."

Jude[8]

VV. 5-7

Though you already know all this, I want to remind you that the Lord delivered his people out of Egypt, but later destroyed those who did not believe. And the angels who did not keep their positions of authority but abandoned their own home—these he has kept in darkness, bound with everlasting chains for judgment on the great Day. In a similar way Sodom and Gomorrah and the surrounding towns gave themselves up to sexual immorality and perversion. They serve as an example of those who suffer the punishment of eternal fire.

Jude provides three examples of God's righteous judgment. First the case of some members of Israel (Numb. 14:2ff.; 32:10-13); secondly the rebellious, fallen angels, and thirdly the cities of Sodom and Gomorrah.

As we have already noted, the sin and fate of the angels is a common theme in Jewish apocalyptic. In fact the expression "for judgment on the great Day" is found in 1 Enoch 10:6; 16:1; 22:4,10,11; 97:5; 103:8. Further, the fate of Azazel, a chief angel, is described in terms of his being thrown into darkness and being covered with darkness (1 Enoch 10:4-5), and other fallen angels are described as being bound until the end of all generations (10:15).

The expression "punishment of eternal fire" refers to that eternal fire awaiting the devil and fallen angels (1 Enoch 67:4ff.; Rev. 19:20; 20:10) of which the fiery destruction of the cities of the plain is a symbolic picture.

Revelation

14:9-11

A third angel . . . said in a loud voice: "If anyone worships the beast and his image and receives his mark on the forehead or on the hand, he, too, will drink of the wine of God's fury, which has been poured full strength into the cup of his wrath. He will be tormented with burning sulphur in the presence of the holy angels and of the lamb. And the smoke of their torment rises for ever and ever.

The beast is the Roman Empire with all its satanic power including caesar-worship. Here is a fierce warning to those who fail in the time of trial and submit to the worship of the emperor. The doom of the apostate and their punishment from God is presented in words which recall the judgment on Sodom and Gomorrah—"Abraham saw dense smoke rising from the land, like smoke from a furnace" (Gen. 19:28), and which also echo Isaiah 34:8-10:

> "For the LORD has a day of vengeance . . . Edom's streams will be turned into pitch, her dust into burning sulphur; her land will become a blazing pitch! It will not be quenched night and day; its smoke will rise for ever."

Further, their punishment is seen by the Lord Jesus and the holy angels. This thought is similar to that expressed in 1 Enoch: "In the last days there will be the spectacle of the righteous judgment upon them (the cursed) before the righteous for ever, for evermore" (27:3). And, "they will burn before the righteous and sink before the holy" (48:9).

19:20

> The beast and the false prophet were thrown alive into the fiery lake of burning sulphur.

The Roman emperor, empire, and their organization and priesthood for caesar-worship are doomed, for the judgment of God upon them is sure, and it is a judgment like that meted out to Sodom and Gomorrah.

20:10

> The devil who deceived them was thrown into the lake of burning sulphur, where the beast and false prophet had been thrown.

This describes the final doom of Satan, after the hostile forces under his leadership have been consumed with fire from heaven (v. 9).

20:14-15

> Then death and Hades were thrown into the lake of fire. The lake of fire is the second death. If anyone's name was not found written in the book of life, he was thrown into the lake of fire.

The voracious monsters who have themselves devoured so many are in the end themselves destroyed; death and Hades will be no more after the last judgment, for the "second death" (= Gehenna, the lake of fire) will have replaced them as far as the wicked are concerned. "Second death" is that spiritual death (= loss of the gracious presence of God) experienced by the wicked after the final judgment. It is also mentioned in 2:11 and 21:8.[9]

Obviously in the book of Revelation we encounter evocative imagery which has roots in both the Old Testament and intertestamental literature. While it points to hell as both a place (a lake) and a state (death), it does not provide literal descriptions. Rather it gives terrible warnings of the doom awaiting the wicked in the context of providing powerful promises of the joy and reward awaiting the faithful and righteous. And much the same may be said of what we read in 2 Peter and Jude. There is certainty of judgment and of punishment for the devil and his angels. Those who behave as did the fallen angels deserve the fate prepared by God for those angels. Yet the nature of the doom is presented in imagery (eternal fire, destruction) which evokes a sense of dread and fear but provides no precise description of its nature and duration.

The Lake of Fire

Notes

[1] For the concept of wrath (*orgē* and *thumos*) see *The New International Dict. of New Testament Theology*, Vol. 1., 105-13.

[2] For death (*thanatos*) see NIDNTT, Vol. 1., 430-41.

[3] For inheritance (*klēronomia*) see NIDNTT, Vol. 2., 295-303.

[4] For anathema (*anathēma*) see NIDNTT, Vol. 1., 413-18.

[5] For *phthora* (= ruin, destruction, perdition, corruption) see NIDNTT, Vol. 1., 467-470.

[6] For *olethros* (= destruction, ruin, death) see NIDNTT, Vol. 1., 465-66.

[7] See further R. Bauckham's comments on this passage in *Jude, 2 Peter*, Waco, Texas, 1983.

[8] See further Bauckham's excellent commentary on Jude.

[9] G. B. Caird, *The Revelation of St. John the divine* (New York, 1966) explains that being thrown into the lake of fire, which is the second death, meant extinction, total oblivion, and annihilation, (186-87, 258-60). However, George Beasley-Murray, *The Book of Revelation*, Grand Rapids, 1981, claims that the lake of fire does not signify extinction in opposition to existence but rather torturous existence in the society of evil in opposition to life in the society of God (304).

Summary

God exists; therefore, heaven as his creation exists. God is the God of grace and mercy; therefore, the new order of the kingdom of heaven of the age to come will surely exist. Jesus and his apostles and evangelists did not doubt the existence of heaven now (i.e. "above") and its future existence as the dominating reality of the new, perfect and sinless cosmos, where fellowship with God will be enjoyed by all. They urged people to turn from their selfish and evil ways, to avoid divine wrath and to be drawn towards God and heaven. However, in describing heaven either as "above" or "yet to come," they necessarily used symbol, image, simile, and metaphor. While these point to heaven as both a place and a state, they do not provide any precise, scientific or literal description of it.

God is a just Judge whose holiness is like a consuming fire; therefore, hell will surely exist for those whom his holy nature excludes from his presence and with whom he cannot have true fellowship and communion. Jesus and his apostles and evangelists did not doubt the existence of hell as a dreadful and horrendous state and place where there was a complete absence of any gracious relationship with God. They warned people to avoid the destiny of the devil and evil angels by repenting and believing the Gospel. The imagery they used was taken from fearful realities in this world, and while it does not provide an accurate account of the cosmology or geography of hell, it does highlight its terrible and desperate nature.

It is important, especially for literally-minded and scientifically-oriented westerners, to grasp that the biblical teaching on heaven and hell is via pictures, images, symbols, similes, and metaphors. It is God's truth in a particular literary form, and this form must always surely be remembered when this truth is put to use either in sermons or in doctrinal statements. In Part 2 we shall notice some of the efforts within the Church over the centuries to interpret this language and use it for doctrinal purposes.

· PART TWO ·

Historical and Theological Overview

·CHAPTER·
6

Death, the Intermediate State, and Judgment

In examining the teaching of Jesus we observed that he had not a little to say about the universal, final judgment at the end of the present age. "All the nations will be gathered before the Son of Man and he will separate the people one from another as a shepherd separates the sheep from the goats" (Matt. 25:32). The same emphasis is found in the Letters of the New Testament, culminating the vision of "a great white throne" with the dead "great and small, standing before the throne" in order to be judged and appropriately rewarded (Rev. 20:11-12). Because of this scriptural teaching our creeds declare that Christ "will come again to judge the living and the dead" (Apostles' Creed) and also that "He will come again in glory to judge the living and the dead and his kingdom will have no end" (Nicene).

As the primitive and early Church came to terms with the delay in the Parousia and accepted the obvious fact that many of the faithful believers would certainly die and be buried before the end of the present age, it had to adjust its eschatological teaching. While the belief in God's future judgment executed by the Son of Man was retained, the result of that assize was effectively brought forward to the moment of death. Thus it was emphasized that a relationship which a person had with God and the Church at the point of death determined his or her everlasting destiny, since "where" he went immediately after death reflected the future verdict. Though this adjustment helped to make sense of the delay of the Parousia, it also, at the same time, raised to greater prominence the interim period between the judgment at death and the final judgment at the Parousia. Obviously the latter was seen as confirming the verdict already given and also adding to it in terms of providing a new immortal body in which to enjoy the full communion of saints and the vision of God.

Generally speaking, the Greek (Eastern) Church showed a healthy reluctance to speculate about this interim period and, while praying for the souls of those who had died as baptized Christians, sought to preserve the idea of final and determinative judgment for the Parousia. In contrast the Latin (Western) Church not only prayed for those who had died as baptized Christians but also gradually developed, in the later patristic and medieval periods, a doctrine of the intermediate state which included the way to heaven via purgatory. Both the Greek and Latin approaches were based on the idea of the conscious existence of human beings as "souls" or "real persons" or "substantival selves." In contrast there were minority groups who held that there is no conscious existence between death and the Parousia, and they followed suggestions in Scripture and called this state psychopannychy, soul-sleep. Such teaching has continued in Protestantism, to which we shall shall return below.

Our task in this chapter is (a) to note how death has been understood in the Christian tradition, (b) to trace the origin and development of the doctrine of purgatory, (c) to explain the orthodox Protestant view of the intermediate state, (d) to comment upon the doctrine of soul-sleep, and (e) to state the orthodox Protestant teaching on the final judgment.[1]

Death

Much has been said and written about the supposed distinction between the so-called "Semitic totality concept" of man as a unitary being and the Greek dualist view which divides the human being into body and soul. Put in such stark contrast the former is then associated with the resurrection of the body, as the result of God's gracious action, and the other is associated with the natural immortality of the soul. It is, of course, wrong to assume that in the Old Testament there is no indication of self-identity, self-awareness, and self-consciousness through memory and inner experience (all of which point to what we may call "soul"). And it is false to assume that all Greek thinking about what happened at death was dominated by belief in the immortality of the soul (Stoics held that the individual was absorbed by death into the cosmic process, and the Epicureans taught that the individual was totally dissolved at death—cf. Acts 17:32).

Thus while the early Christians inherited from Jesus and the Old Testament scriptures a strong sense of man as a unitary being, they also could think in terms of the separation of soul and body (as is suggested by Wisdom 3:1 and 4 Maccabees; and cf. Matt. 10:28 and Luke 12:4-5). In other words they had the concepts and the vocabulary to think and speak of a person existing through both death and the interim period until the Parousia, without a physical body. Certainly as the early Church made more use of Greek philosophy in its apologetics and theology, it spoke more readily and naturally both of the body and soul and of the immortality of the soul. However, there remained the question whether this immortality of the soul (= substantival self) was natural (having been so created) or was by grace (dependent in a particular way on the word and action of God in Christ). The majority opinion from the later patristic period through to the nineteenth century seems to have been that immortality belongs to the human soul because in creating each soul God created it immortal.

Though physical death is obviously a part of the cycle of life as we observe it in nature, its universal existence in the human race is interpreted in biblical teaching and in traditional theology as the tragic and unnecessary result of human sin and satanic strategy. Only the incarnation, death, resurrection, ascension, and parousia of the Son of God can effectively halt, reverse, and transform the power and finality of death; and not until the end of the age will the victory of the Son of God be wholly manifested.

Thus the separation of body and soul at death creates an abnormal situation. Unlike the angels who are pure spirit, the soul/human person functions normally and fully only in, through, and with a body—be it a physical or a spiritual body. So in a certain sense, the interim period between death and the Parousia represents an "inferior" or "diminished" mode of existence when compared with the final state after the Parousia and general resurrection of the dead. In other words we would expect that the experience of God and the transcendent realities of heaven and hell will be necessarily limited because of the nature of the human receptivity, as well as by the fact that the culmination of God's purposes has not yet arrived and thus the communion of the saints has not reached its final form. Nevertheless, much church teaching over the centuries has treated the intermediate state as if it were, to all intents and purposes, identical with the final state. This is probably best explained in terms of the heavy commitment to the doctrine of the natural immortality of the soul and the viewing of the soul as the essence of whatever it is to be human.[2]

In both Protestantism and Roman Catholicism, as both followed the medieval teaching, death has been seen as that which brings an end to our condition as pilgrims. With physical death human destiny is fixed irrevocably. No person can any longer influence that destiny any more than the runner who has finished the mile race can continue the race when the mile is completed. It is the outward sign of an inward finality; with death a person attains his or her final mode of being; his development ceases, for when the soul leaves the body it has already taken all the decisions it could have taken. So after death the person remains the same but is constituted in a different way: He is a disembodied self but the same self. He awaits the resurrection of the body.

At death there is, according to traditional teaching, a particular judgment which anticipates the universal judgment at the Parousia. The dead do not ascend into eternal life or descend into everlasting darkness simply in virtue of the state of their souls. God in Christ passes a verdict upon them, and thus it is for each person as if the Parousia occurred for him alone. For Protestants the possibilities of this particular judgment are two—heaven or hell; for Roman Catholics they are heaven (with purgatory as a non-direct route into heaven) and hell (with possibly the limbo for unbaptized children, who suffer the results of original but not actual sin).[3]

In much modern theology, as we shall note below, death has not been afforded the finality that it has held in traditional, orthodox theology. Especially within the last century various reasons have been offered to suggest that there will be opportunity after death for most if not all people to respond afresh or anew to the grace of God in Jesus Christ.

Before looking at the Roman Catholic doctrine of purgatory, it is salutary to observe that a possible weakness in the exposition of traditional orthodoxy can be that the vital emphasis goes where the writers of the New Testament do not actually place it—i.e., at death instead of at the Parousia. This changed emphasis for judgment can have the effect of diminishing the sense of the corporate, cosmic, and teleological dimensions of the last judgment and, in practice, simply making the last judgment into a reason for living righteous lives.[4] In this way of thinking, final judgment is effectively and only particular judgment at each person's death, with the final judgment as the public and universal proclamation of all the individual judgments already executed. Such doctrines as the "sleep of the soul" and "conditional immortality" (on which we shall comment in the chapter on hell) at least have the merit of placing the vital emphasis upon the final judgment at the end of the age. Later in this chapter we shall return to this discussion to note how the relation of individual and final, universal judgment have been reconciled.

Purgatory[5]

In 1563 the Roman Catholic Council of Trent approved the *Decree concerning Purgatory*, which was intended to have pastoral implications, while confirming the received doctrine. It reads:

> Whereas the Catholic Church, instructed by the Holy Spirit, has, from the Sacred Writings and the ancient tradition of the Fathers, taught, in sacred Councils, and very recently in this ecumenical Synod, that there is a Purgatory and that the souls there detained are helped by the suffrages of the faithful, but principally by the acceptable sacrifice of the altar—the holy Synod enjoins on bishops that they diligently endeavor that the sound doctrine concerning Purgatory, transmitted by the holy Fathers and sacred Councils, be believed, maintained, taught, and everywhere proclaimed by the faithful of Christ.[6]

We shall look later at the biblical texts (Sacred Writings) and the teaching of the patristic period (ancient tradition of the Fathers). Here it may be noted that the Councils which had set forth the doctrine of purgatory were the second Council of Lyons (1274) and the Council of Florence (1439). Earlier in the work of the Council of Trent the doctrine of purgatory (understood as the place where the debt of temporal punishment is discharged by those in the process of being justified) was assumed in the *Decree concerning Justification* (1547).[7]

The teaching of Trent is restrained when compared with the contents of the sermons of some medieval preachers, whose imagination served to exaggerate aspects of their theology, e.g., of purifying fire.[8] It is, however, in accord with the noblest representation of purgatory—that of the poet, Dante Alighieri in his remarkable *Purgatorio,* written about 1319 and extremely important in the popularization of the doctrine of purgatory and its related piety.[9] In Roman Catholic teaching, purgatory was understood as the state, place, or condition which will exist until the last judgment; here the souls of those who die in a state of grace (but not yet free from all imperfection and sin) make expiation for unforgiven venial sins or for the temporal punishment due to venial and mortal sins that have already been forgiven; thus they are purified before they enter into heaven, the only place of exit from purgatory.[10] The classic expositions are by Robert Bellarmine (d. 1621) and Francisco de Suarez (d. 1617).

1. *The origin and development of the doctrine,* Through the doctrine that came to be called purgatory was within the tradition of the western Church from the patristic period, the word, *purgatorium,* was not used until 1254 in an official letter sent by Pope Innocent IV to the Greek Church. Purgatory referred to a "temporary fire, where slight and minor sins (which could not have been forgiven on earth through penance) are purged." The same letter also states that the souls in purgatory may be helped by the suffrages of the Church on earth.[11]

Moving back through eight centuries, we can see the origins of this concept. In the writings of Augustine, bishop of Hippo, we find both the idea of the temporary fire of purification/purgation and the commendation of suffrages for the dead. This outstanding theologian prayed for his own mother, Monica, that she would rest in peace with God with her husband, who had died before her, and he also prayed that God would inspire readers of his book to pray for her, when they attended the Eucharist (*Confessions* 9:13.34-37). He fully accepted the liturgical tradition not only of praying for baptized Christians who had died but also of offering the Eucharist to God, especially for the dead in Christ.

Augustine's references to a period of purification by fire after death are of a tentative rather than a dogmatic kind and are usually reflections on 1 Corinthians 3:10-15, a much-quoted text in later discussions of purgatory. Of the fire mentioned in this text, Augustine wrote: "The fire may be experienced perhaps only after this life, or both in this life and hereafter, or in this life only and not hereafter" (*City of God*, 21:26). He held that this fire of purgation worked only on "lesser" sins (venial sins had not yet been defined) and that, while it was a fire that the faithful might pass through in the sufferings of this life, it was also a fire that some might expect to experience intensely after death and before entry into heaven. It was these two points that were developed in the centuries after the death of Augustine in 430.

It may be asked, "Since Augustine was such a careful student of the Scriptures, where did he find scriptural support both for prayers for the dead and for purging fire after death before entry into heaven?" Three chief biblical texts were cited by Augustine, his predecessors, colleagues, and successors. It must be remembered that the Bible is always understood and interpreted in a specific situation and within a tradition of meaning. Thus, since the Church prayed weekly for the Christian dead, the Bible was understood as supporting this practice, directly or indirectly. And since a very serious view was taken of sin committed after the "washing of holy baptism," to die without either having been forgiven for that sin or having done the appropriate penance for it posed a theological problem; purgation after death en route for heaven seemed to solve it.

The first biblical text was certainly a *scriptural* source for the Church of the patristic period even if it is not so for Protestants today. It is 2 Maccabees 12:39-46, found in the Apocrypha.

On the following day, since the task had now become urgent, Judas and his men went to gather up the bodies of the slain and

116

bury them with their kinsmen in their ancestral tombs. But under the tunic of each of the dead they found amulets sacred to the idols of Jamnia, which the law forbids the Jews to wear. So it was clear to all that this was why these men had been slain. They all therefore praised the ways of the Lord, the just judge who brings to light the things that are hidden. Turning to supplication, they prayed that the sinful deed might be fully blotted out. The noble Judas warned the soldiers to keep themselves free from sin, for they had seen with their own eyes what had happened because of the sin of those who had fallen. He then took up a collection among all his soldiers, amounting to two thousand silver drachmas, which he sent to Jerusalem to provide for an expiatory sacrifice. In doing this he acted in a very excellent and noble way, inasmuch as he had the resurrection of the dead in view: for if he were not expecting the fallen to rise again, it would have been useless and foolish to pray for them in death. But if he did this with a view to the splendid reward that awaits those who had gone to rest in godliness, it was a holy and pious thought. Thus he made atonement for the dead that they might be freed from this sin. (NAB)

Here we find both prayers for the dead and the offering of an atoning sacrifice on their behalf. Thus a scriptural proof was available both for prayer and the Eucharist being offered for the Christian dead.

The second text was Matthew 12:32 and is part of the teaching of Jesus concerning blasphemy against the Holy Spirit:

Anyone who speaks a word against the Son of Man will be forgiven, but anyone who speaks against the Holy Spirit will not be forgiven, either in this age or in the age to come.

What was of interest here was the possible suggestion that forgiveness might occur in the age to come. Certainly this is not directly taught, but in the general mood described above such a conclusion was not irrational.

The third text was 1 Corinthians 3:10-15, in which Paul

insists that Christ is the foundation of the Church, and thus all must be built upon him and be worthy of him. The language recalls Malachi 2-3, especially 3:1-3. Paul wrote:

> By the grace God has given me, I laid a foundation as an expert builder, and someone else is building on it. But each one should be careful how he builds. For no one can lay any foundation other than the one already laid, which is Jesus Christ. If any man builds on this foundation using gold, silver, costly stones, wood, hay or straw, his work will be shown for what it is, because the Day will bring it to light. It will be revealed with fire, and the fire will test the quality of each man's work. If what he has built survives, he will receive his reward. If it is burned up, he will suffer loss; he himself will be saved, but only as one escaping through the flames. (NIV)

We now understand that Paul intended that the "fire" belonged to the Last Judgment at the end of this age, but as suggested by Augustine and developed by those who followed him, the "fire" was also taken to be applied by God to baptized but imperfect souls after death and before their entry into heaven and the arrival of the final judgment. In this interpretation the Latin West differed from the Greek East, where it was generally agreed that the "fire" belonged uniquely to the last judgment (a fact, however, which in no way hindered their offering of prayer for the Christian dead).

During the thirteenth century there is an acceleration in the commitment of the western Church to the idea of purgatory. There is the scholastic exposition of the doctrine (e.g., by Aquinas in the Supplement to the *Summa Theologiae*) in the context of such themes as the distinction between mortal and venial sin, prayer for the dead, and indulgences; there is the new Feast of All Souls (the commemorating of the souls of the faithful departed) and there is the greater use of indulgences, given a boost by the famous Jubilee Indulgence of 1300, which made provision for the promotion from purga-

tory to heaven of certain classes of the faithful dead. Therefore, it is not surprising that doctrinal definitions are provided
by Councils (Lyons, 1274; Florence, 1439) and that there was
a flowering of a piety which was geared to the virtual certainty that after death almost all the baptized would spend a
certain period in the process of purification.[12]

Such developments were open to distortion, exaggeration,
and abuse, and it can be seen that much of the negative pro-
test of the Protestant Reformation was directed against not
only the doctrine of purgatory (for lack of basic support in the
New Testament) but also the abuses and excesses connected
with belief in it. In 1523 Zwingli asserted that, "The true
Holy Scriptures know nothing of a purgatory after this life."[13]
Though wholly rejected by Protestants, the Roman Catholic
Church reaffirmed its commitment to the doctrine at the
Council of Trent (as we noted above) and at the same time
made great efforts to remove some of the obvious abuses connected with it. Even so, the careful explications of the teaching of Trent did not convince Protestant theologians. Only in
the mid-nineteenth century, with the birth of the Anglican
Anglo-Catholic movement, did the practice of praying for
the dead and belief in purgatory enter in a small but significant way into the Protestant Church.[14]

2. *Recent Expositions of Purgatory.* It is not surprising to find
in the post-Vatican II Roman Catholic Church a variety of
approaches to purgatory, ranging from the traditional and orthodox to the open-ended and liberal.

(a) The orthodox doctrine is clearly presented in the sub-
stantial article on purgatory in the *New Catholic Encyclopedia*
by R. J. Bastian. He admits that "in the final analysis, the
Catholic doctrine on purgatory is based on tradition not
Scripture," though it is in harmony with the Bible. Further,
he explains that underlying this doctrine are two presuppositions: (1) the great difference between mortal sin, which unforgiven leads to hell, and venial sins, which do not cause

damnation but still need to be forgiven; (2) the punishment due to sin is not always forgiven along with the guilt of sin; hence this punishment is to be paid by the forgiven sinner either in this life or in the next before he can enter heaven. However, Bastian recognizes that questions relating to the punishments of purgatory are more obscure than the question of the existence of purgatory.

The length of time spent in purgatory is not known in advance, for "the separated soul no longer lives in the time of this world, but in *aevum,* where duration is not measured in days and years." Thus in our understanding of time the punishment/suffering could be over in a moment or last for a longer period. It is best to think of the punishment in both its negative (deprivation of the beatific vision of God) and positive aspect (some actual experience of divine chastisment). As to the purpose of suffering, the soul in purgatory has to be set free of three basic defects: the guilt of venial sin, the inclination towards sin, and the temporal punishment due to sin. Nevertheless, purgatory is a sphere and place of grace where there is certitude of salvation and anticipation of the pure vision of God.

(b) Michael Schmaus, formerly professor in Hamburg, may be called an orthodox Roman Catholic theologian who has a particular sensitivity to Protestant and Greek Orthodox teaching. Thus in his chapter on purgatory in his book, *Justification and the Last Things,* he attempts the presentation of purgatory in an attractive dress. It is, he explains, "to be understood as a way of life after death wherein man has a particular relation to God." His decision for life with God was made on earth but he is not yet ready for the unmediated, face-to-face dialogue with God. Though sin has been forgiven, maturity of character and personality have not yet been attained, and therefore further grace is needed:

When a person arrives after death at the full realization of what God means for him and is at the same time aware that he is not yet ready for face-to-face dialogue with God, the experience is full of pain. It is the ardent love he now feels for God that causes him to feel this anguish.

However, as purification proceeds he feels a greater joy, and through true and perfect love he becomes his true and proper self, mature in the grace of God.

Schmaus rejects the idea of punishment by fire (real or metaphorical) since he sees fire as a symbol of the Holy Spirit as the purifier of souls. However, he is happy with both the practices of prayer for the faithful dead and of applying indulgences to the dead, for they can help, through God's ordination, in the process of purification in purgatory.

(c) Anton van der Walle, the Prior of the Dominicans in Brussels, is less committed to orthodox and traditional Roman Catholic ideas on purgatory than the German, Michael Schmaus. In fact the former believes that the development of the doctrine in the Western Church has been too legalistic and juristic, with too much emphasis upon undergoing punishment and providing satisfaction. He thinks that the Greek patristic emphasis upon purifying mercy is better. In *From Darkness to the Dawn*, he writes:

> We may see purgatory as an encounter with God in which God gives risen humanity the chance to make amends for wrong doing towards him and creation; it is not just a demand of divine righteousness . . . but a revelation of his immensely great mercy.

He holds that the resurrection occurs at death and is thus able to write in this way of the experience of purifying mercy immediately after death. Further he is happy with the definition of Karl Rahner that heaven, purgatory, and hell are not places; rather they are different designations for God.[15] Heaven is God who has finally become our own; purgatory is God who goes through us to purify us, while hell is God as the opportunity we have lost. Finally we may note that he thinks that prayer for the dead is wholly appropriate because of solidarity within the body of Christ, the inter-connection and communion between the members of the one Christ.

In terms of the interpretation of the presence of fire in purgatory, there has been a major swing away from understanding this as real fire, instead explaining fire in terms of purification by the presence and power of the Holy Spirit.

The intermediate state in Protestant teaching[16]

All the Protestant Reformers rejected the doctrine of purgatory but continued to hold to the view of an intermediate state between individual death and the last judgment. John Calvin actually wrote against the doctrine of the unconscious "sleep" of the soul in his book, *Psychopannychia*. His view was that the intermediate state is to be understood in terms of both blessedness (or misery) and expectation of greater fulfillment. Thus the blessedness or the misery is incomplete and provisional. The clarity of the Protestant view will be communicated best by selections from Confessions and Catechisms as well as from liturgical texts.

In the *Scottish Confession of Faith* (1560), chapter xvii we read:[17]

The chosen departed are in peace, and rest from their labours: not that they sleep and are lost in oblivion as some fanatics hold, for they are delivered from all fear and torment, and all the temptations to which we and all God's chosen are subject in this life, and because of which we are called the Kirk Militant. On the other hand, the reprobate and unfaithful departed have anguish, torment, and pain which cannot be expressed. Neither the one nor the other is in such sleep that they feel no joy or torment, as is testified by Christ's parable in Luke xvi and his words to the thief; and the words of the souls crying under the altar, "O Lord Thou that art righteous and just, how long shalt thou not revenge our blood upon those that dwell in the earth?"

Interestingly this chapter is given the title "Immortality." The texts quoted are Luke 16:19ff.; 23:43 and Revelation 6:9, which are all obviously understood as pointing to the intermediate state.

Six years later the authors of the *Second Helvetic Confession* (1566) wrote as follows in chapter xxvi:[18]

> *The State of the Soul Departed from the Body.* For we believe that the faithful, after bodily death, go directly to Christ, and, therefore, do not need the eulogies and prayers of the living for the dead and their services. Likewise we believe that unbelievers are immediately cast into hell from which no exit is opened for the wicked by any services of the living.

No scriptural texts are given in this Confession. Nearly a century later in answer to their question, "What is the communion in glory with Christ, which the members of the invisible church enjoy immediately after death?" the Westminster divines answered thus in the *Larger Catechism* (1647):[19]

> The communion in glory with Christ, which the members of the invisible church enjoy immediately after death, is, in that their souls are made perfect in holiness, and received into the highest heavens, where they behold the face of God in light and glory, waiting for the full redemption of their bodies, which even in death continue united to Christ, and rest in their graves as in their beds, till at the last day they be again united to their souls. Whereas the souls of the wicked are at their death cast into hell, where they remain in torments and utter darkness, and their bodies kept in their graves, as in their prisons, till the resurrection and judgment of the great day.

The texts quoted for heaven are Hebrews 12:23; 2 Corinthians 5:1,6,8; Philippians 1:23 (compared with Acts 3:21 and Ephesians 4:10); 1 John 3:2; and 1 Corinthians 13:12. For hell those quoted are Luke 16:23-4; Acts 1:5; Jude 6,7.

Doctrine is usually communicated more by the content of the services of worship than by confessions and catechisms. If we look at the services for the burial of the dead produced by the Protestant churches we find that they are written for the faithful (or on the charitable supposition that all die as Christians), and they assume that the soul has gone or is going immediately to heaven. For example, the Burial Service of the *Book of Common Prayer* of the Church of England, published in 1549 (and reissued in the 1662 edition) has this prayer:

> Almighty, God, with whom do live the spirits of them that depart hence in the Lord, and with whom the souls of the faithful after they are delivered from the burden of the flesh, are in joy and felicity, we give thee hearty thanks that it had pleased thee to deliver this our brother/sister out of the miseries of this sinful world.

At the same time there is the expression of hope for the resurrection of the body at the last day.

The orthodox Protestant position has held and holds that at death God's judgment comes into effect and that where the disembodied person spends the intermediate state is determined by where he will be after the last judgment. Thus in popular speech people are said to have gone to heaven or to hell at their death. However, since the late nineteenth century, a growing number of theologians and Christian leaders have taught that death is not necessarily followed by immediate judgment and that there will probably be an opportunity, especially for those who never properly heard the good news of the kingdom, to respond to the grace of God before the final judgment. This is rarely argued on the basis of biblical exegesis (i.e., the citing and explaining of specific passages) but is more usually a deduction from beliefs about the character of God, e.g., his justice and love. And of course a strong case can be made out that people do not have equal opportunities either to hear or to respond to the gospel in this life before death. What of millions in China, of babies who die in infancy, of the mentally retarded and those who for not obvious fault of their own do not hear the authentic message concerning Jesus, the Christ.

Writing in 1918, the Scottish theologian J. H. Leckie observed that "the majority of evangelical teachers at the present day hold some form of the doctrine that is commonly called 'Future Probation.'" Leckie was well read in German divinity, and he certainly had in mind such well-known names as I. A. Dorner (1809-84), Julius Müller (1801-78) and F. J. Delitzsch (1813-90), all of whose primary works had been translated into English. He also referred to F. L. Godet (1812-1900), the Swiss biblical scholar, as holding to "Future Probation." Leckie explained:

> Their argument is that, since the New Testament asserts that there is no salvation except through Christ, it implies that every soul of man must have an opportunity of accepting him. But this again involves the conclusion that the ministry of the Saviour continues beyond the grave. If he is to draw all men to himself, then he must be lifted up in the sight of all men; and those who have not seen him in the days of their flesh must be enabled to see him hereafter. If this be not true, then the teaching of the Apostles is meaningless: their claim that he is the appointed Saviour of all men is altogether vain.[20]

With increasing discussion of the fate of souls after death not only in Christian theology but also in the teaching of the great religions of the world, the word "pareschatology" has been introduced to denote discussion of the "next to last things," that which happens in the intermediate state before the final consummation. In his much-used book, *Death and Eternal Life*, John Hick has a chapter on pareschatology in which he delves into various religions and makes his own suggestion based on "insights" from a variety of religious traditions. Brian Hebblethwaite also use the term in his book

The Christian Hope, but he seeks to fill it with Christian content. Like many before him Hebblethwaite believes that considerations of theodicy and moral and religious plausibility, not to mention the revealed nature of God, cause the theologian to envisage further opportunities beyond the grave for those people who were denied genuine opportunity of receiving God's love and grace on earth.

In particular, Hebblethwaite is conscious that the "main problem for a Christian theology of religion has been that of doing justice both to the spirituality and faith manifest in all the great religions and to the uniqueness and finality of Christ as summed up in the Christian doctrine of the Incarnation." Thus he writes: "To postulate further salvific encounters with God in Christ beyond the grave is to envisage space and time for non-Christians to come to recognize the human face of God uniquely in the risen Christ and to find in him the universal focus of God-man encounter, after which, in their different ways the religions of the world have been feeling".[21]

To find top-grade theologians of recent decades who follow the Protestant Confessions in their basic theology of death and the intermediate state is not easy. One such is the late G. C. Berkouwer of the Free University in Amsterdam, who discusses this question in his *The Return of Christ*, chapter two. However, Berkouwer is conscious of (a) the tension between individual and corporate salvation raised by the twofold expectation of encountering Christ individually at death and then with others at the Parousia, and (b) the danger of building theories of the intermediate state which rest on a particular doctrine of man as immortal or of the relation of time and eternity. Further, he has nothing to say about the position of those who die without having confessed Christ as their Savior. Rightly, in our judgment, he sees the central thrust of the position of the Reformers as being that a believer is "in Christ" before death, in death, and after death. Thus as

Paul declared we are convinced that "neither death nor life" nor anything else in the creation "will be able to separate us from the love of God that is in Christ Jesus our Lord" (Rom. 8:38-9). Thus being "in Christ," the believer looks with Christ toward the fulfillment of God's purposes in the Parousia, the Last Judgment, and the New Creation.

Another theologian within the Reformed tradition, who, like Berkouwer, admires Calvin and Barth, is Thomas F. Torrance of Edinburgh University. He differentiates between "the time of the new creation" of the exalted Christ and that time in which we live on this earth. Thus of the death of the believer he writes:

> When the believer dies, he goes to be with Christ and is in his immediate presence, participant in him and made like him. That is to each believer the *parousia* of Christ to him. Yet when this is regarded on the plane of history and of the on-going processes of the fallen world, the death of each believer means that his body is laid to sleep in the earth, waiting until the redemption of the body and the recreation of all things at the final *Parousia*. Looked at from the perspective of the new creation there is no gap between the death of the believer and the *parousia* of Christ, but looked at from the perspective of time that decays and crumbles away, there is a lapse in time between them.

But how do you think these together? asks Torrance. His answer is "by thinking of them exclusively *in Christ*, in the one Person of Christ in whom nature and divine nature are hypostatically united, and in whom our human existence and history are taken up into his divine life."[22] This position, arrived at from a Christological perspective and a particular view of God and time, is much the same as that arrived at by biblical exegesis, especially the exegisis of 2 Corinthians 5:1-10, by both Dr. Murray Harris and Professor F. F. Bruce: They believe that at death the believer is clothed in his new resurrection body of glory.[23]

While the teaching of Torrance, Harris, and Bruce, together with others who think as they do, cannot be called heresy, it certainly does not seem to give sufficient prominence to the fact of the End and the great consummation of God's salvific work. The position of Berkouwer is to be preferred in that, whatever its difficulties, we do have to accept the fact of the intermediate state and the expectation therein for the Parousia and the new order. As Calvin said, there is blessedness and anticipation.[24]

Soul-sleep

The description of the state of physical death as "sleep" is found in a variety of languages and cultures. It is the kind of metaphor that springs to mind to describe the state of a dead physical body, especially when that body lies with eyes closed and in an apparent state of peaceful contentment. Therefore it is not surprising that sleep is used figuratively in the Old Testament, New Testament, and intertestamental literature.

In the Septuagint the phrase *ekoimēthē meta tōn paterōn autou* (he slept with his fathers) is fairly common in 2 Kings and Chronicles (see e.g., 2 Kings 14:16,22,29; 15:7,22,38). It means that he died an honorable death. The NIV translates the Hebrew as "he rested with his fathers." In 1 Enoch "sleep" refers to the intermediate state between physical death and the resurrection: "And the righteous will rise from sleep and wisdom will rise and will be given to them" (91:10); "And the righteous man will rise from sleep, will rise and will walk in the path of righteousness, and all his paths and his journeys will be in eternal goodness and mercy" (92:3).

In the New Testament the following chief texts use sleep in a figurative sense:

Matt. 27:52, "saints who had fallen asleep were raised" (RSV). NIV has "had died."

128

John 11:11-12, "Lazarus has fallen asleep."

Acts 7:60, "When Stephen had said this, he fell asleep."

Acts 13:26, "David fell asleep; he was buried with his fathers."

1 Cor. 15:6,18,20, "Those who have fallen asleep in Christ." (See also 7:39; 11:30)

1 Thess. 4:13,14,15, "those who have fallen asleep in Christ."

2 Peter 3:4, "Ever since our fathers fell asleep" (RSV). NIV has "died."

In these verses the verb is *koimaō* (passive), the same verb as used in the Septuagint to render *sakab* (Hebrew, to sleep).

In general these texts have been interpreted in the Church over the centuries as referring to death and the person who has died being at peace with the Lord. However, there have been those within the Church (that is, mainline churches/ denominations) as well as within certain sects (e.g., Jehovah's Witnesses and Mormons) who have developed a doctrine of soul-sleep (= psychopannychy) from these texts. Usually they have denied the immortality of the soul, argued that sleep refers to the cessation of conscious existence, and pointed to the last judgment as the moment when eternal destiny is decided. Thus soul-sleep has been understood either as extinction or as a kind of suspension of existence in anticipation of the last day.[25] As we have noted Calvin saw this teaching as a denial of the scriptural emphasis that the believer dies in the Lord, for death cannot separate him from his Lord. Further, we may note that the Confession of Faith of the Church of England, *The Forty-Two Articles* of 1553 (later shortened into the *Thirty-Nine Articles* of 1562), contained in Article 40 a condemnation of soul-sleep:

They which say that the souls of such as depart hence do sleep, being without all sense, feeling or perceiving until the day of judgment, or affirm that the souls die with the bodies, and at the last days shall be raised up with the same, do utterly dissent from the right belief declared to us in holy Scripture.[26]

Whatever precisely is the nature of the intermediate state, it is not the suspension of existence: It is life in Christ.

Having referred to John Calvin several times, it will be appropriate to close this section with a disclaimer on soul-sleep from his *Institutes of the Christian Religion* (Book III, chap. xxv, sec. 6):

> Now it is neither lawful nor expedient to inquire too curiously concerning our souls' intermediate state. Many torment themselves overmuch with disputing as to what place the souls occupy and whether or not they already enjoy heavenly glory. Yet it is foolish and rash to inquire concerning unknown matters more deeply than God permits us to know. Scripture goes no farther than to say that Christ is present with them, and receives them into paradise (cf. John 12:32) that they may obtain consolation, while the souls of the reprobate suffer such torments as they deserve. What teacher or master will reveal to us that which God has concealed? Concerning the place, it is no less foolish and futile to inquire, since we know that the soul does not have the same dimension as the body. The fact that the blessed gathering of saintly spirits is called "Abraham's bosom" (Luke 16:22) is enough to assure us of being received after this pilgrimage by the common Father of the faithful, that he may share the fruit of his faith with us. Meanwhile, since Scripture everywhere bids us wait in expectation for Christ's coming, and defers until then the crown of glory, let us be content with the limits divinely set for us: namely, that the souls of the pious, having ended the toil of their warfare, enter into blessed rest, where in glad expectation they await the enjoyment of the promised glory, and so all things are held in suspense until Christ the Redeemer appear. The lot of the reprobate is doubtless the same as that which Jude assigns to the devils: to be held in chains until they are dragged to the punishment appointed for them (Jude 6).

Final Judgment

The Protestant Confessions of the sixteenth and seventeenth centuries provide more detail concerning the End than do the Ecumenical Creeds, but what they say is only an extension of the teaching of the Creeds. In the famous Lutheran Confession, the *Augsburg Confession* (1530) we read in chapter xvii:

> It is also taught among us that our Lord Jesus Christ will return on the last day for judgment and will raise up all the dead, to give eternal life and everlasting joy to believers and the elect, but to condemn ungodly men and the devil to hell and eternal punishment.
>
> Rejected, therefore, are the Anabaptists who teach that the devil and condemned men will not suffer eternal pain and torment.

Here we have Parousia, Judgment, and Heaven/Hell. The "Anabaptists" were such men as Hans Denck and Melchior Rinck.[27] In a later chapter we shall examine universalism.

Six years after the Lutheran Confession came the Swiss Reformed, or Calvinistic, Confession, the *First Helvetic Confession,* which in Chapter xi, "Concerning Christ the Lord and What we have through Him," has these two paragraphs:[28]

> This Lord Christ, who has overcome and conquered death, sin and the whole power of hell, is our Forerunner, our Leader and our Head. He is the true High Priest who sits at God's right hand and always defends and promotes our cause, until He brings us back and restores us to the image in which we were created, and leads us into the fellowship of his divine nature.
>
> We await this Lord Jesus to come at the end of the world as the true, righteous Judge, who will pass a true judgment upon flesh which he has raised to judgment. He will lead the godly and believing into heaven, and will condemn and thrust unbelievers into eternal damnation.

Here again we have the Parousia of the heavenly Lord, the raising of the dead, their judgment, and the final destinies of heaven and hell.

In 1560 the *Scottish Confession* was published, and this too dealt with the Parousia in the same chapter as the Ascension and Session of the Lord Jesus. In chapter xi we read.[29]

> We believe that the Lord Jesus shall visibly return for this Last Judgment as he was seen to ascend. And then, we firmly believe, the time of refreshing and restitution of all things shall come, so that those who from the beginning have suffered violence, injury, and wrong, for righteousness' sake, shall inherit that blessed immortality promised them from the beginning. But, on the other hand, the stubborn, disobedient, cruel persecutors, filthy persons, idolators and all sorts of unbelieving, shall be cast into the dungeon of utter darkness, where their worm shall not die nor their fire be quenched.

Here we have no specific reference to the Resurrection but instead the words "the time of refreshing and restitution of all things." This recalls Acts 3:19-21, where the words "refreshing" and "restitution" are both found in the KJV. They point to the "new heavens and new earth" and the dwelling there of the righteous in their resurrection bodies of glory. Further, hell is described in terms of the dungeon (Rev. 20:7), utter or outer darkness (Matt. 8:12), and the imagery of the last verse of Isaiah's prophecy (66:24).

The final quotation is from the *Westminster Confession of Faith* (1647), chapter xxxiii, "Of the Last Judgment." In the previous chapter belief in the resurrection of the dead had been affirmed, and so it is not specifically mentioned in this chapter which reads:[30]

> I. God hath appointed a day, wherein He will judge the world, in righteousness, by Jesus Christ, to whom all power and judgment is given of the Father. In which day, not only the apostate angels shall be judged, but likewise all persons that have lived upon earth shall appear before the tribunal of Christ, to give an account of their thoughts, words and deeds; and to receive ac-

cording to what they have done in the body, whether good or evil.

II. The end of God's appointing this day is for the manifestation of the glory of his mercy, in the eternal salvation of the elect; and of his justice, in the damnation of the reprobate, who are wicked and disobedient. For then shall the righteous go into everlasting life, and receive the fulness of joy and refreshing, which shall come from the presence of the Lord: but the wicked, who know not God, and obey not the Gospel of our Lord Jesus Christ, shall be cast into eternal torments and be punished with everlasting destruction from the presence of the Lord and from the glory of his power.

III. As Christ would have us to be certainly persuaded that there shall be a day of judgment, both to deter all men from sin; and for the greater consolation of the godly in their adversity: so will He have that day unknown to men, that they may shake off all carnal security, and be always watchful, because they know not at what hour the Lord will come; and may be ever prepared to say, Come Lord Jesus, come quickly, Amen.

Among the verses from Scripture cited in the footnotes are Acts 3:19 and 2 Peter 3:11, both of which in context refer to the new order of reality called the "new heavens and new earth."

In the next two chapters we shall be looking at the everlasting order of heaven and hell, as well as at the nature of the resurrection bodies of those who dwell therein. Here it is necessary only to make some comments on the relation of personal, particular judgment and the universal final judgment. Particularly judgment deals only with one person at a time with reference to his conscience and life and relates only to his eternal destiny. The general, universal judgment involves everyone who has ever lived and is the last judgment in that it is not followed by any other and its sentence endures as eternally present to all wherever they are, and it never becomes obsolete. The Judge at each judgment is Christ, acting on behalf of the Father.

For God himself the general and last judgment is a public vindication of his providence and grace in the world from its creation until its regeneration. For those who are "in Christ," their Savior, Mediator, and Intercessor (and against whom God has no wrath for all that could separate them from God has been removed by Christ), the judgment is a time of joyous triumph: They share with Christ in judging of the peoples, and their faithfulness and good works are shown to be the fruit of grace and to have contributed to the growth of the kingdom of God on earth. For those who have rejected the offer of forgiveness and life in Jesus, the judgment is an exposure of their sins and the evil effects they had upon others, as well as the harm done to the progress of the Gospel. They are brought to see the futility of their lifelong opposition to grace and to see how they deserve God's wrath and punishment.[31]

Notes

[1] For the biblical material see *NIDNTT*, vol. 1, 429ff.; also P. Cotterell, *What the Bible Says About Death*, Wheaton, Illinois, 1979. For a philosophical introduction see John Hick, *Death and Eternal Life*, London, 1976.

[2] See further James P. Martin, *The Last Judgment in Protestant Theology from Orthodoxy to Ritschl*, Edinburgh, 1963, chapters 2 and 3.

[3] On Limbo see the article, "Limbo," in the *New Catholic Encyclopedia*.

[4] Martin, *Last Judgment*, 43ff.

[5] I have found Jacques Le Goff, *The Birth of Purgatory*, Chicago, 1984, illuminating and helpful on both the origins of the doctrine and its development up to the end of the middle ages.

[6] In P. Schaff, *Creeds of Christendom*, Grand Rapids, 1977, Vol. 2., 199.

[7] Ibid., 89ff.

[8] For descriptions see Goff, Purgatory, 133ff.

[9] Dante's trilogy on *Hell*, *Purgatory*, and *Heaven* is available in the Penguin Classics series, translated and edited by Dorothy L. Sayers.

[10] Venial sins are offenses against God which do not deprive the

sinner of the inner grace of sanctification. They have been called "daily sins" and "light sins." Mortal sins are those offenses against God which destroy sanctifying grace and cut the soul off from the grace of God. They have been called "deadly" and "grave" sins.

[11] Goff, *Purgatory*, 283-84.

[12] Ibid., 326ff. for a fascinating section on "Wills and Obituaries."

[13] This is article 57 of *Zwingli's Sixty-Seven Articles* (1523) printed in *Reformed Confessions of the Sixteenth Century* (ed. Arthur Cochrane), Philadelphia, 1966, 42-43. See also the *French Confession* (1559), article xxiv, and the *Second Helvetic Confession* (1566), chapter xxvi, for further Calvinist condemnations of purgatory; both are in Cochrane, op. cit., 153 and 295. For condemnations in the Lutheran confessions see *The Book of Concord: The Confessions of the Evangelical Lutheran Church* (ed. T. G. Tappert, Philadelphia, 1959), 184,185,199,202,205,207,209,261,266,294,306,307. Finally see Article xxii of the *Thirty-Nine Articles* of the Church of England, found in *Creeds of the Churches* (ed. J. H. Leith, Richmond, Virginia, 1973), 274.

[14] For details see Geoffrey Rowell, *Hell and the Victorians*, Oxford, 1974, 99ff.

[15] Rahner's views may best be gathered from his *Foundations of Christian Faith* (1976) and the articles on eschatology in *Sacramentum Mundi* as well as in his multi-volume *Theological Investigations*.

[16] For biblical studies see A. A. Hoekema, *The Bible and the Future*, Grand Rapids, 1978, chap. 9, and Karel Hanhart, *The Intermediate State in the New Testament*, Franeker, Holland, 1966.

[17] Cochrane, *Reformed Confessions*, 175.

[18] Ibid., 295.

[19] *The Confession of Faith and Larger and Shorter Catechisms*, Edinburgh, 1967, 174-77, Q. 86.

[20] J. H. Leckie, *The World to Come and Final Destiny*, Edinburgh, 1918, 94-95.

[21] Brian Hebblethwaite, *The Christian Hope*, London, 1984, 219.

[22] T. F. Torrance, *Space, Time and Resurrection*, Edinburgh, 1976, 102.

[23] Murray Harris, *Raised Immortal*, 159ff., and F. F. Bruce, "Paul on Immortality," *Scottish Journal of Theology*, Vol. 24 (1971) 457-471, and *1 and 2 Corinthians*, London, 1971, 204.

[24] The text of Calvin's *Psychopannychia* may be found in *Tracts*

and Treatises, trans. H. Beveridge, Grand Rapids, 1958, Vol. 3, 413-490.

[25] See further A. A. Hoekema, *Four Major Cults*, Grand Rapids, 1963, 110-11, 135-36, 265-66, 293-94, 345-359. B. F. C. Atkinson, *Life and Immortality* (privately printed and published in England in 1967) argues both for conditional immortality and the sleep of the soul. This is an important book since Atkinson was a leader in the evangelical movement in Cambridge University for many years. See further John W. Wenham, *The Goodness of God*, Leicester, 1974, 39-41.

[26] The text is in E. C. S. Gibson, *The Thirty-Nine Articles of the Church of England*, London, 1898, 88 in both Latin and English.

[27] For the text and reference to these names see *Book of Concord*, 38.

[28] Cochrane, *Reformed Confessions*, 103.

[29] Ibid., 171.

[30] *The Confession of Faith*, 124-26.

[31] For further details see H. Heppe, *Reformed Dogmatics*, Grand Rapids, 1978, 703ff., where Calvinistic divines are quoted. See also A. A. Hodge, *Outlines of Theology*, London, 1972, 574-75.

·CHAPTER·
7

Heaven

As has already become clear, in traditional Roman Catholic and Protestant theology, talk about entering and being in heaven belongs not only to the age after the Parousia but also to the intermediate state. In Protestant teaching the believer, justified by faith and sanctified by the Spirit, goes via death immediately into heaven; in Roman Catholic teaching the martyrs and saints go via death immediately into heaven, while the ordinary faithful, who need further purifying, go via purgatory to heaven. Thus any suggestion that Christian believers do not enjoy the true vision of God in the intermediate state was seen as heresy.

Take the well-known case of Pope John XXII. In 1331 he preached a series of sermons in Paris. He did not claim to be speaking *ex cathedra* but to be expressing his own theological opinions. As a "private" theologian he claimed that those who die and go to heaven do not enjoy the true and full vision of the Triune God (thereby fulfilling the Beatitude, "they shall see God") but enjoy only the vision of Christ's glorified humanity in the intermediate state. The Franciscans arose to defend the Pope's views while the Dominicans resolutely opposed him. There was a fierce theological controversy and it is claimed that on his death-bed John XXII retracted his opinion.[1] It was left to his successor, Benedict XII, to set forth the traditional and orthodox position in his Constitution, *Bene-*

dictus Deus (1336). According to this authoritative document, the souls of the faithful departed see, on entering heaven, the true vision of the Triune God. Here, in a rather literal translation, is part of the text:[2]

> According to the general disposition of God, the souls of all the saints who departed from this world before the passion of our Lord Jesus Christ, and also those of the holy apostles, martyrs, confessors, virgins, and other faithful who died after receiving the holy baptism of Christ—provided they were not in need of any purification when they died, or will not be in need of any when they die in the future, or else, if they then needed or will need some purification, after they have been purified after death—and again the souls of children who have been reborn by the same baptism of Christ or will be when baptism is conferred on them, if they die before attaining the use of free will: all these souls, immediately *(mox)* after death and, in the case of those in need of purification, after the purification mentioned above, since the ascension of our Lord and Saviour Jesus Christ into heaven, already before they take up their bodies again and before the general judgment, have been, are and will be with Christ in heaven, in the heavenly kingdom and paradise, joined to the company of the holy angels. Since the passion and death of the Lord Jesus Christ, these souls have seen and see the divine essence with an intuitive vision and even face to face, without the mediation of any creature by way of object of vision; rather the divine essence immediately manifests itself to them, plainly, clearly, and openly, and in this vision they enjoy the divine essence. Moreover, by this vision and enjoyment the souls of those who have already died are truly blessed and have eternal life and rest. Also the souls of those who will die in the future will see the same divine essence and will enjoy it before the general Judgment.

The centrality of the beatific vision, the *visio dei*, for all thinking about the nature of heaven, is obvious here: In fact the beatific vision is central to all medieval and Roman Catholic accounts of heaven. Apostles, saints, and martyrs of the Christian era, together with the faithful of the old covenant (having previously been in *limbo patrum*[3] until the Ascension) and along with the purified faithful from the Church Militant, enjoy the true vision of the Triune God both in the intermediate state and after the Parousia.

The Protestant Confessions are equally clear that the vision of God is enjoyed by the disembodied souls of the righteous after death. This is how the *Westminster Confession of Faith* (1647), chapter xxxii puts it:[4]

> The bodies of men, after death, return to dust, and see corruption: but their souls, which neither die nor sleep, having an immortal subsistence, immediately return to God who gave them: the souls of the righteous, being made perfect in holiness, are received into the highest heavens, where they behold the face of God, in light and glory, waiting for the full redemption of their bodies.

Scriptural texts cited for these lines are Genesis 3:19; Acts 13:36; Luke 23:43; Ecclesiastes 12:7; Hebrews 12:23; 2 Corinthians 5:1,6,8; Philippians 1:23 (with Acts 3:21 and Ephesians 4:10).

Because it is held that heaven is enjoyed by the believer both as a disembodied soul and as a resurrected person with an immortal body, descriptions of heaven in the prose and poetry, confessions and hymnody of both Roman Catholics and Protestants do not always distinguish between heaven as it is *now* and as it will be *then*. Of course heaven is heaven and its essence and nature cannot change: What it is and will be for the redeemed was constituted and fixed by the arrival and coronation of Jesus, incarnate Son, in his Exaltation to the Father's right hand.[5] Forever he is and will be the only Mediator between God and human kind. Even so, the external relations (as we might call them) of heaven will change. *Now* heaven stands in a temporary and ambivalent relation to a universe and age infected by sin, suffering, and death and dominated by Satan, who opposes God's holy purposes: This universe is under God's judgment and will be wholly purified. *Then,* that is after the Parousia, heaven will have a unifying, controlling, and harmonious relation to the new order/ universe/age, being at it very center. *Now* heaven is populated by the angels, who are pure spirits, and by righteous, disembodied souls, whose number is ever growing; *then* heaven, at the heart of the new cosmos, will be populated by the angels and by the total number of the elect in their resurrected bodies of glory. And it is very important to remember that the incarnate Son, the enthroned Lamb, is always and forever the same.

As we come to look at the teaching of the Church we shall need to be aware of these two "phases" of the glorious, ongoing life of heaven even though we shall discover that much writing on heaven (e.g., of the beatific vision) applies just as much to *now* as to *then.* In this chapter we shall examine characteristics of heaven. First, we shall note how the nature of the resurrection body of the righteous has been described. Second, we shall look at the brief but profound description of heaven provided by St. Augustine of Hippo. Then we shall explain what is meant by the beatific vision in various Christian traditions. Finally, we shall provide a general description of heaven as it appears in various writings.

Resurrection bodies

In the Apostles' Creed the faithful confess as individuals: "I believe in the resurrection of the body." The last four words translate the Greek *sarkos anastasin,* or the Latin *carnis resurrectionem,* which literally translated are "resurrection of the flesh," meaning the total physical body of a human being.

The reason the word "flesh" (*sarkos* and *carnis*) was chosen instead of "body" (*sōma* and *corpus*) is twofold. The earliest of Christian theologians in the second century wanted to affirm that there would be a real and true resurrection of the self-same body that died, and that in that same body a person would be judged by Christ for what he had achieved in that body. But later we find that there was controversy in Christian circles caused by some who denied the resurrection of the dead. This caused Justin Martyr to write: "If you meet the people who describe themselves as Christians . . . but dare blaspheme the God of Abraham, of Isaac and of Jacob, and affirm that there is no resurrection of the dead . . . do not recognize them as Christians."[6] Tertullian of North Africa aimed his *De Resurrectione mortuorum* (*ca.* 210) against Gnostics who denied the physical resurrection of bodies.

This emphasis upon the resurrection of the flesh, that is, the same body, continues through the patristic, medieval, and Reformation periods. For example, the *Larger Catechism* (1647) in its answer to Q87 states: "The self-same bodies of the dead which were laid in the grave, being then again united to their souls for ever, shall be raised up by the power of Christ."[7] John Pearson, Bishop of Chester, wrote this in his classical *Exposition of the Creed* (1659):[8]

> I am fully persuaded of this as of a most necessary and infallible truth, that as it is appointed for all men once to die, so it is also determined that all men shall rise from death, that the souls separated from our bodies are in the hands of God and live, that the bodies dissolved into dust, or scattered into ashes, shall be recollected in themselves, and reunited to their souls, that the same numerical bodies which did fall shall rise, that this resuscitation shall be universal, no man excepted, no flesh left in the grave, that all the just shall be raised to a resurrection of life and all the unjust to a resurrection of damnation; that this shall be performed at the last day when the trump shall sound; and thus I believe THE RESURRECTION OF THE BODY.

Though they insisted on the resurrection of the self-same body, patristic, medieval, and Protestant theologians also emphasized, as we shall now see, that this body will be wholly transformed into an immortal body of glory, as also the whole universe is also totally renewed and regenerated by the redemptive power of God (Rom. 8:19ff.).

Not a few medieval theologians indulged in what we today regard as unnecessary speculation about the characteristics and properties of the resurrection body of the righteous. Thomas Aquinas believed (based on Ephesians 4:13) that the human body would have the development appropriate to the age of thirty, which was that of the risen Christ in his full, human maturity. Thus those who were younger and those who were older would be resurrected and transformed to look like what they were when they were thirty or what they would have looked like had they reached the age of thirty. The point that he and others were making was that the resurrection-body is the perfect counterpart to the glorified soul, and thus it has to be perfect and complete in every respect.[9]

In essentials there is agreement among medieval, Protestant, and Roman Catholic theologians as to the "marks" of the spiritualized (= wholly amenable to the Spirit's action) and glorified (= imbued and filled with the glory of Christ) resurrection bodies. They insist that each resurrection body will be endowed with immortality and incorruptibility, indestructibility, subtlety, agility, and clarity. They arrived at these descriptions particularly by reflecting upon Paul's teaching in 1 Corinthians 15 and upon the accounts of the Transfiguration of Jesus in the Gospels, as well as the descriptions of heaven we noted in chapters 1,2, and 3 in Part One. They also came to these "marks" by reflection upon the relation of the perfected and glorified soul to the new body. Thus 'marks' which belong to the soul are transferred to the body because the body has become a perfect instrument for the soul. The marks of subtlety and agility, when applied to Christ on earth after his resurrection, point to his ability to pass through closed doors and sealed tombs as well as his power to move at will to any part of the universe in an instant. Thus applied to the faithful in heaven they also point to their ability as filled with the Spirit and wholly perfected to be present in any part of the new creation at any time—i.e., they can discharge a cosmic function. The mark of clarity is the ability to see into things and to see them as they really are; further, as an embodied soul it is the ability to see God. Thus in the new creation glorified humankind truly has dominion.[10]

At the general resurrection human bodies are restored to life and equipped with new senses, qualities, and characteristics. The sphere in which the redeemed, glorified righteous live is also recreated for the new humanity so that it is truly in all respects the kingdom of God. Of this new order, the Protestant confessions only supply hints; for example, the *Westminster Confession* merely states that "then shall the righteous go into everlasting life, and receive that fulness of joy and refreshing, which shall come from the presence of the Lord" (chap. xxxiii).[11] And the *Heidelberg Catechism* (1563) had this answer to Q.123:[12]

> "Thy kingdom come." That is, so govern us by thy Word and Spirit that we may more and more submit ourselves unto thee. Uphold and increase thy church. Destroy the works of the devil, every power that raises itself against thee, and all wicked schemes thought up against thy holy Word, *until the full coming of thy kingdom in which thou shalt be all in all.*

Here there is the theme of the fulness of the kingdom, taken primarily from the Synoptic Gospels, and that of God himself being all in all, taken primarily from Paul's teaching (e.g., 1 Cor. 15:28).

The reticence of the Protestant Confessions concerning the new, everlasting order, cosmos, and kingdom may be explained in various ways—e.g., the hesitation concerning the interpretation of Revelation 20-21 (Calvin, the great biblical expositor, never wrote a commentary on this book); the fact that the Ecumenical creeds speak only of the communion of the saints, the resurrection of the body, and life everlasting; and the great emphasis within theology on heaven as primarily the beatific vision (and thus of heaven as primarily, though not only) of a state. However, there is no lack of discussion concerning the origin of that new heaven and earth in the Lutheran and Calvinist theologians of the seventeenth century. They debated whether the new order would be *creatio ex nihilo* or would be through the renewal of the old order. Further, they exhibit a certain tension between thinking of heaven as place and as state: This is because their primary definition of heaven is in terms of the beatific vision, which the disembodied soul also enjoyed (as we have seen) in the intermediate state.[13]

The words of A. A. Hoekema are worth quoting:

> The Bible assures us that God will create a new earth on which we shall live to God's praise in glorified, resurrected bodies. On the new earth, therefore, we hope to spend eternity, enjoying its beauties, exploring its resources, and using its treasures to the glory of God. Since God will make the new earth his dwelling place, and since where God dwells there heaven is, we shall then continue to be in heaven while we are on the new earth. For heaven and earth will then no longer be separated as they are now, but they will be one. But to leave the new earth out of consideration when we think of the final state of believers is greatly to impoverish biblical teaching about the life to come.[14]

The theme of cosmic renewal in and by Christ was often referred to in the debates at the Second Vatican Council. In *The Pastoral Constitution on the Church in the Modern World* (1965), often known by its opening Latin words, *Gaudium et Spes*, we read this in section 39:[15]

We know neither the moment of the consummation of the earth and of man, nor the way the universe will be transformed. The form of this world, distorted by sin, is passing away and we are taught that God is preparing a new dwelling and a new earth in which righteousness dwells, whose happiness will fill and surpass all the desires of peace arising in the hearts of men. Then with death conquered the sons of God will be raised in Christ and what was sown in weakness and dishonor will put on the imperishable: charity and its works will remain and all of creation, which God made for man, will be set free from its bondage to decay.

We have been warned, of course, that it profits man nothing if he gains the whole world and loses or forfeits himself. Far from diminishing our concern to develop this earth, the expectancy of a new earth, should spur us on, for it is here that the body of a new human family grows, foreshadowing in some way the age which is to come. That is why, although we must be careful to distinguish earthy progress clearly from the increase of the kingdom of Christ, such progress is of vital concern to the kingdom of God, insofar as it can contribute to the better ordering of human society.

When we have spread on earth the fruits of our nature and our enterprise—human dignity, brotherly communion and freedom—according to the command of the Lord and his Spirit, we will find them once again, cleansed this time from the stain of sin, illuminated and transfigured, when Christ presents to his Father an eternal and universal kingdom of truth and life, a kingdom of holiness and grace, a kingdom of justice, love and peace. Here on earth the kingdom is mysteriously present; when the Lord comes it will enter into its perfection.

This is a fine statement built upon the conviction that the new order of the age to come will both fulfill and transcend this present age.

Not only Roman Catholics but also evangelicals have in recent times emphasised the hope of a new order. In the *Lausianne Covenant* (1974), a document which is primarily about

evangelism and mission in God's world, these words describe
the Christian hope.

> We reject as a proud, self-confident dream the notion that man
> can ever build a utopia on earth. Our Christian confidence is
> that God will perfect his kingdom, and we look forward with ea-
> ger anticipation to that day, and to the new heaven and earth in
> which righteousness will dwell and God will reign forever.
> Meanwhile, we rededicate ourselves to the service of Christ and
> of men in joyful submission to his authority over the whole of our
> lives.[16]

Augustine on heaven

In closing the last book of his mammoth treatise, *The City
of God*, Augustine of Hippo wrote: "Vacabimus et videbimus,
videbimus et amabimus, amabimus et laudabimus. Ecce quod
erit in fine sine fine."[17] This may be translated: "There [i.e., in
our future life in heaven in our resurrection bodies of glory]
we shall rest and we shall see; we shall see and we shall love;
we shall love and we shall praise. Behold what shall be in the
end shall not end." We shall take the verbs in this marvelous
description of heaven one by one.

1. *Vacabimus* (we shall rest). Augustine was thinking of the
teaching in the Letter to the Hebrews concerning the Sabbath rest of God into which Christ and his people enter (see
chapter four for our presentation of the texts). After six days
spent in creating the world, God rested on the Sabbath day.
That is, God took time to contemplate what he had made and
rejoice in his creation—just as a painter stands back and looks
at his painting when he is finished. Further, after his great
work of atonement on Good Friday, Jesus rested in the tomb
on Holy Saturday (the Great Sabbath) as he enjoyed the work
of the new creation and looked upon the travail of his soul
with satisfaction. Thus the rest of God into which the faithful

enter now (in part) and wholly (at the end) is not a kind of stagnation or inertia; it is not boredom but a perfection of life and holy contentment that we have no words adequate to describe it.

In his *De Catechizandis Rudibus* Augustine advises on giving catechetical instruction when many may be joining the church for worldly advantage. If a candidate desires to become a Christian "for the Rest to come," then take him at his word, and teach him the faith, saying, "I rejoice for you that in all the perilous storms of this world you have considered the security that is real and certain." Later Augustine states:

> He who will become a Christian for the sake of the everlasting happiness and rest perpetual promised after this life to the saints, that he may not go into eternal fire with the devil, but enter with Christ into His eternal Kingdom, he is a Christian indeed—wary in all temptation, lest he be corrupted by prosperity or broken by adversity, moderate and self-restrained in abundance of worldly goods, brave and patient in tribulations. Such a man will yet go forward and attain a better state, in which he will love God more than he fears hell.[18]

The better state will become the final state in which "we shall have leisure to be still and we shall see that he is God," and seeing that he is God, we shall be filled with him when he will be all in all.

2. *Videbimus* (we shall see). In the penultimate chapter of the last book of the *City of God*, Augustine discussed the *visio dei* and whether we shall see God with the "physical eyes" of the new resurrection bodies as well as with the inward eye of the spirit/heart. He believed that the vision of God will be such that he will be seen and known by the whole person, not only in a direct manner but also via his new creation.

> It is possible, it is indeed most probable, that we shall then see the physical bodies of the new heaven and the new earth in such

147

a fashion as to observe God in utter clarity and distinctness, seeing him everywhere present and governing the whole material scheme of things. . . . Perhaps God will be known to us and visible to us in the sense that he will be spiritually perceived by each of us in each one of us, perceived in one another, perceived by each in himself; he will be seen in the new heaven and earth, in the whole creation as it then will be; he will be seen in every body by means of bodies, wherever the eyes of the spiritual body are directed with their penetrating gaze.[19]

Then will be fulfilled the text, "Blessed are the pure in heart for they shall see God."

3. *Amabimus* (we shall love). Augustine has much to say about God's love for man and man's love for God. John Burnaby's masterly study of Augustine's spirituality is appropriately titled *Amor Dei*. God himself, as Augustine never tired of saying, is the reward of the love which he infuses and inspires in the hearts of the regenerate. Pure love of God is nothing else but the longing for the vision of God, since nothing that God can promise has any worth apart from himself: "For God is to be loved freely and the soul cannot rest save in that which it loves. But eternal rest is only given to it in the love of God, who alone is eternal." Thus in that rest

we shall feel need no longer, and therein shall be our happiness. For we shall be filled, filled with our God, who Himself will be to us all that our longings make us count most desirable here. . . .

He who has given the promise is himself the end of our longing. He will give himself, because he has given himself [in the Incarnate Son's death]. He will give his own immortal being to our immortality, because he gave himself as mortal to our mortality.

Thus in this affirmation that God himself is the reward of the love which he inspires and that love accepted is love gained, Augustine not only makes his special contribution to our thinking on the love of God but shows how love for God in this life is marvelously magnified and rewarded in the life to come.[20]

Some of the insights of Augustine are developed in a short but profound treatise on the love of God by Bernard of Clairveaux (1090-1153).[21] The life of love is divided into four stages: (1) the love of a man for himself is the realism accepted by the commandment to love others as you love yourself; (2) the loving of God for what he is towards human beings as sinners; (3) the love of God for God's sake because he is supremely lovable; (4) the love of self only for the sake of God. Though this scheme—self for self; God for self; God for God; self for God—may appear artificial, it does contain a profound estimate of the love of human beings for God. The first three stages belong to the life of imperfection as there is growth in holiness; the last stage can be realized only in heaven within the beatific vision and in a resurrection body of glory. In this final state God is love supremely and alone, for the love of self is only for the greater glory of God. Thus heaven in a community of love originating in and being fulfilled in the love of God—Father, Son, and Holy Spirit.

During the middle ages the Dominicans and Franciscans debated this question: Will our complete happiness in heaven consist *primarily* in knowing God (i.e., seeing him) or in loving him? The Dominicans insisted that the primary aspect of heaven was knowing God through the beatific vision, thereby following their great teacher Thomas Aquinas, while the Franciscans argued that it was loving God and thus sharing in the divine love of the Holy Trinity, as Augustine had written. Their debate as to whether the supreme ecstasy is more affectional than intellectual was really a waste of time, for they debated that which they had not experienced and could know only in part. It is a question we need not face; however, this debate is put in some sort of context by the final verb used by Augustine.

4. *Laudabimus* (we shall praise). At the beginning of the last chapter of the *City of God* he wrote:

> How great will be that felicity, when there will be no evil, where no good will be withheld, where there will be leisure for the praises of God, who will be all in all. What other occupation could there be in a state where there will be no inactivity of idleness, and yet no toil constrained by want? I can think of none. And this is the picture suggested to my mind by the sacred canticle, when I read or hear the words, "Blessed are those who dwell in your house; they will praise you for ever and ever!"

Concerning the task of a Christian on earth, Augustine had already written, "What will be your work, but to praise him you love, and to make others share your love of him?" Concerning the praise of God, which has a highly paradoxical character, we may reiterate the comment of Dr. E. L. Mascall:

> The sole justification for praising God is that God is praiseworthy. We do not praise God because it does us good, though no doubt it does. Nor do we praise him because it does him good, for in fact it does not. Praise is thus strictly *ecstatic*, in the sense that it takes us wholly out of ourselves; it is purely and solely directed upon God. . . . Praise is entirely directed upon God. It takes our attention entirely off ourselves and concentrates it entirely upon him. It neither does God any good, nor does it profess to do so. Its sole and sufficient justification lies in the fact that God is praiseworthy. And that is the only justification that it needs.[22]

In one of his printed sermons Augustine states:

> Because our vision of the True will be without satiety, in perpetual delight, because our contemplation will have the perfect assurance of immediacy—kindled, then, by the love of Very Truth, cleaving to him in the pure embrace of spirit, our spirit's voice will praise him and say, "Alleluia." Uplifting one another to the same praise, in most fervent love to one another and to God, all

the citizens of that city will say, 'Alleluia,' inasmuch as they will say, "Amen."[23]

Thus Christians' activity will be the praise of God—Alleluia—and the acceptance of his will and word—Amen (so be it). "Let us rest assured, my brethren," he said on another occasion.

We shall not be wearied by the praise of God, nor by his love. If your love should fail, so would your praise; but if love will be everlasting, because the beauty of God will be uncloying, inexhaustible, fear not that you will lack power ever to praise him, whom you will have power ever to love.[24]

This rest, vision, love, and praise will be both personal and communal. God will be a common vision, possession, and reward, for he will be enthroned in every heart. "The peace of the heavenly city is the perfectly ordered, perfectly united fellowship in the fruition of God and of one another in God."[25] In this *fruitio dei*, the fulfillment of one another in God, "the hearts of all will be transparent, manifest, luminous in the perfection of love."[26]

Thus the experience of resting, seeing, loving, and praising will continue forever within the heavenly city of God at the center of the new heaven and earth. And "what shall be in the End, shall not end," for such is what the creed highlights in the words, "I believe in the life everlasting."

Visio Dei—seeing God in heaven

Christians have consistently looked forward to the *visio dei* in heaven. Their hope has been fueled by the beatitude, "Blessed are the pure in heart for they will see God" (Matt. 5:8), the warning, "without holiness no one will see the Lord" (Heb. 12:14), the promise, "We shall see him as he is"

(1 John 3:2), and the Old Testament presentation of both the invisibility of God (Exod. 33:20; cf. 1 Tim. 6:16 and Heb. 11:27) and his visibility through his self-revelation in grace (Exod. 33:18ff. and 34:29ff.). How often have the words of Paul been quoted: "Now we see but a poor reflection; then we shall see face to face" (1 Cor. 13:12)! What the "face to face" will mean has been glimpsed not only by the mystics but by the many thousands who have entered into the secret place and prayed to their heavenly Father in secret.

Since God is Eternal Spirit and not a massive physical reality, no attempt to describe the *visio dei* has been easy. The popular way has been to cite biblical texts, explain them by simple illustrations taken from common experiences of "seeing" and "knowing," and then invite people to use their imagination to think of that seeing and knowing of God which brings perfect happiness. As Calvin wrote:

> For though we very truly hear that the kingdom of God will be filled with splendor, joy, happiness and glory, yet when these things are spoken of, they remain utterly remote from our perception, and, as it were, wrapped in obscurities, until that day comes when he will reveal to us his glory, that we may behold it face to face.

And also:

> If the Lord will share his glory, power, righteousness with the elect—nay, will give himself to be enjoyed by them and, what is more excellent, will somehow make them to become one with himself, let us remember that every sort of happiness is included under this benefit.[27]

As the beatific vision (that vision of God which brings perfect happiness to the elect) was explained in theological terms in the patristic and medieval periods, such expressions as *fruitio dei* (fruition of fulfillment of the hope of full salvation and redemption and seeing God "face to face") and *sicuti est* (from the Vulgate of 1 John 3:2, "as he is") were used, and to them was added the expression, *visio per essentiam* (i.e., seeing God as he essentially is as Triune). Originally the "seeing of God" was understood in terms of the God who fully reveals himself to the body of Christ who are the faithful in heaven: the *sicuti est* originally was conceived in the dynamic biblical sense of the God of grace who discloses himself in Christ, the incarnate Son, to the limits that redeemed humanity can receive and appropriate. Yet when *sicuti est* was interpreted by *visio per essentiam*, as happened in the late medieval period, then the God who will be seen is not the God who discloses himself fully as Creator, Lord, and Savior but rather the God as he is in himself as holy Trinity. Because it was recognized that such a vision of God was different than seeing God in, through, and by Christ, as the self-revealer, theologians proposed that a further gift of grace was necessary for these who entered heaven. They called this extra gift the *lumen gloriae* ("light of glory" from Psalm 36:9, "In thy light we see light").

It was claimed that this knowledge of God is the true fulfillment of this spiritual nature of man. As the Council of Vienne (1311) insisted it is an absolutely supernatural endowment. As such, it is the fruit of a sublime, final and permanent enlightment of human nature. And, as the mystics, Tauler and Eckhart explained, this light of glory transfigures and elevates human nature so that by it we know God direct as we know ourselves, not merely as we know another human being.[28]

Though this *visio per essentiam* and *lumen gloriae* became part of orthodox Roman Catholic theology, they are not always emphasized by modern Roman Catholic writers and are generally rejected within the Protestant tradition, which has always sought to maintain the emphasis on the *visio dei* but to interpret it in terms of the biblical *sicuti est* of the God who reveals himself.[29]

Michael Schmaus, has written concerning the *visio dei* in these words:[30]

> The concept of the beatific vision cannot be understood if it is viewed under its objective aspect; it must be seen as the joy-giving, life-giving exchange between God and man wherein man is liberated from all self-seeking and gives himself to God in total openness, and wherein God on his side gives himself to man without any barrier. Although the word vision has an intellectual connotation, this seeing of God must be understood in the biblical sense as an act leading to union. It is a personal, existential occurrence. A personal God cannot be an object at the disposal of man, the creature: he is always the Lord who gives himself, Love who gives himself freely.

Schmaus proceeds to explain that

> it is because man is made in the likeness of God and transformed through his incorporation in Jesus Christ that he is able to attain this vision of the transcendent God. In this process he is not transformed into God but raised to a higher level in his nature as man. This, he states, is what the medieval theologians meant by speaking of the *lumen gloriae*.

The Christocentric emphasis of Schmaus is dominant in Protestant teaching on the *visio dei*. In his exegesis of 1 John 3:2 Calvin equates the vision of Christ in his glorified body with the vision of God: In the consummation believers see God in Christ and are thus transformed into the image of God. "Our glory will not be so perfect as to be able to comprehend the Lord in his absolute Godhead. Even at the last there will remain an impassable distance between himself and us" comments Calvin. The *visio dei* implies fullness of communion and fellowship with God in and through Christ and thus, like Augustine he combines the *fruitio dei* and the *visio dei*. In turn, this means blessedness and complete salvation—

perfect release from sin, death, pain, and sorrow and perfect joy in Christ. It also means participation in the glory of heaven, for the whole of the elect as the church is perfected by being given resurrection bodies of glory and by being united into one people, one body, one temple to praise and magnify the Lord. And all this will occur in the new cosmos, the perfect place and sphere for the new humanity to enjoy the glorious life of heaven. "The end of the glorification of man and the world is the glory of God."[31]

Jonathan Edwards, America's greatest philosopher-theologian of grace, had much to say about heaven and the beautific *visio*. In a sermon on Matthew 5:8 he explained not only what it is to be pure in heart but also the nature of the *visio dei*.[32] Of seeing God in Jesus he said:

> The saints in heaven will behold an outward glory as they are in the human nature of Christ which is united to the Godhead, as it is the body of that person who is God; and there will doubtless be appearances of a divine and inimitable glory and beauty in Christ's glorified body, which it will indeed be a refreshing and blessed sight to see.
>
> But the beauty of Christ's body as seen by the bodily eyes will be ravishing and delightful, chiefly as it will express his spiritual glory. The majesty that will appear in Christ's body will express and show forth the spiritual greatness and majesty of the divine nature; the pureness and beauty of that light and glory will express the perfection of the divine holiness; the sweetness and ravishing mildness of his countenance will exoress his divine and spiritual love and grace.

And he went on to explain the nature of the *visio dei*:

> It is an intellectual view by which God is seen. God is a spiritual being and he is beheld with the understanding. The soul has in itself those powers which are capable of apprehending objects and especially spiritual objects, without looking through the

155

windows of the outward senses. This is a more perfect way of perception than by the eyes of the body. . . . The eye of the soul is vastly more perfect than the eye of the body.

To see God implies the sight of him as glorious and gracious—a vision of the light of his countenance, both as it is understood of the effulgence of his glory and the manifestations of his favor and love.

Edwards proceeded to explain what this intellectual view of God in heaven will be like. It is called "seeing God" (1) because the view will be very direct, as when we see things with the bodily eyes. In heaven God will immediately excite apprehensions of himself. (2) Because the knowledge of God will be most certain, for when people see things with their own eyes they are certain that it is real. In heaven the sight of God will exclude all doubting. (3) Because the apprehension of God's glory will be as clear and lively as when any thing is seen with bodily eyes. (4) Because the intellectual sight which the saints will have of God will make them sensible of his presence, and give them as great an advantage of conversing with him, as the sight of the bodily eyes does an earthly friend. In heaven the souls of the saints will have the most clear sight of the spiritual nature of God. They will behold his attributes and disposition towards them more immediately and with greater certainty than it is possible to see anything in the soul of an earthly friend by his speech and behavior.

Finally Edwards showed that the *visio dei* is also *fruitio dei*, for in seeing God the soul will be wholly fulfilled and made perfectly happy. Seeing God provides and yields a delight suitable to the nature of human beings, and by it they are perfectly fulfilled in their thinking, feeling, and willing. Further, since the glory of God is inexhaustible and eternal, it never ceases to shine and thus the fulfillment and delight of the redeemed people of God is also always maintained at the highest point. "Blessed are the pure in heart for they shall see God."

Heaven—what is it like?

Heaven is both a place and a state, but it is easier to offer a description of it as a state than as a place. As a state heaven will be a profoundly richer experience of God and the communion of saints than can be enjoyed in this age on this earth. As "new heavens and new earth," the age of the kingdom of God will be a created place/sphere, the like of which we have not yet experienced and concerning which we can have the dimmest intimations.[33] Death will be behind (instead of in front of) the population of the kingdom; time and space will not be the same as known here on earth, and relationships will be of a different order. This being so, it is clear that the life of the new humanity in their resurrection bodies of glory can be described only in symbolic terms, that is, with images and language derived from present day-by-day experience in this world, together with the recognition that the symbols cannot be perfectly adequate to the reality of this life in the age to come.

For our summary of what heaven will be like we shall rely upon the summaries provided by a Presbyterian of the nineteenth century and an Anglican of the twentieth century.[34] What heaven—that is the new order after the last judgment— will be like may be put in one sentence, as did A. A. Hodge: "Heaven, *as a place*, is where Christ, the God-Man, is. Heaven, *as a state*, is one of intimate knowledge of him and of the whole Godhead in him, and of fellowship with him." The same writer continues to explain: "Heaven, as the supreme centre of divine revelations and communications through Christ, must pre-eminently bear the characteristics of God. It will be absolutely pure, majestic, holy, noble, in all its elements and characteristics." Yet it will also be perfectly suited for sanctified humanity.

> Heaven, as the eternal home of the divine Man and of all the redeemed members of the human race, must necessarily be thoroughly human in its structure, conditions, and activities. Its joys and activities must all be rational, moral, emotional, voluntary and active. There must be the exercise of all the faculties, the gratification of all tastes, the development of all talent capacities, the realization of all ideals. The reason, the intellectual curiosity, the imagination, the aesthetic instincts, the holy affections, the social affinities, the inexhaustible resources of strength and power native to the human soul must all find in heaven exercise and satisfaction. Then there must always be a goal of endeavour before us, ever future.

Thus the pathway of the redeemed and glorified will always be with Christ Godward.

B. H. Streeter adds further details concerning the idea of heaven. Life in heaven must be thought of as life in a society—the New Jerusalem, the kingdom of God, and the communion of saints: "The most conspicuous feature of that society will be not merely that the exercise of active love will be as possible there as it is on earth but that the love will be of an intenser quality, will lavish itself on a wide range of persons, and will always express itself more freely and in more diverse ways." And there must be work, for did not Jesus say, "My Father is always at his work to this very day, and I, too, am working" (John 5:17). Though the new humanity will enter into God's rest (as Augustine emphasized), it is not the rest of boredom, laziness, or inertia, but that rest which, though it does not bring fatigue and tiredness, involves being a coworker with God himself.

In the third place there will be profound knowledge and thought (related to the *visio dei*). Paul had confessed: "Now I know in part; then I shall know fully even as I am fully known" (1 Cor. 13:12). Love is higher than knowledge, but love will not be without knowledge, and there will be a constant growth in knowledge of God, his creation, his purposes, and his ways. Fourth, there will be the full apprehension and enjoyment of the Beautiful: This is suggested by the apocalyptic visions of Revelation. Then, fifth, heaven will contain humor, that humor which belongs to the true exercise of human nature in human community and which is the spontaneous expression of the joy of living. We give the final word to A. A. Hodge, who wrote:

> The constitution of heaven will be related not only to human nature, redeemed and glorified, but also to angelic nature in all its grades and orders. Christ and the commonwealth of his redeemed kindred after the flesh will be central. But with us all holy intelligences in all their infinite varieties of rank and gifts and functions will be comprehended. Heaven will prove the consummate flower and fruit of the whole creation and of all the history of the universe.

Notes

[1] For the controversy see *History of the Church*, Vol. IV (ed. Hubert Jedin, London, 1980), 313-14, and D. Douie, "John XXII and the Beatific Vision," *Dominican Studies* 3 (1950), 154-174.

[2] The translation is taken from *The Christian Faith: Doctrinal Documents of the Catholic Church* (ed. J. Neuner and J. Dupuis, Bangalore, India, 1973), 624.

[3] See the article on "Limbo" in the *New Catholic Encyclopedia*.

[4] *The Confession of Faith*, 123.

[5] The fact that heaven was changed by the arrival there of the God-Man is not always made clear in theological text-books. However, A. A. Hodge of Princeton Seminary did insist upon this point: "It follows that when, on the evening of Friday, the soul of the then

dead Christ, personally united to his divinity, entered Paradise, he must have irradiated it with a sudden light never seen there nor in all the universe of God before. That one moment consummated heaven and revolutionized the condition of the redeemed for ever. How much more, then, when some forty days afterward, in his completed person, his risen and glorified body united to his glorious soul and Godhead, he ascended and sat down on the right hand of the Majesty on high, must the seats of bliss have been transformed and glorified for ever, and made the central temple and cosmopolitan eye and crown of the universe!" *Evangelical Theology,* Carlisle, PA, 1980, 369.

[6] Cited by J. N. D. Kelly, *Early Christian Creeds,* London, 1960, 164.

[7] *The Confession of Faith,* 175.

[8] J. Pearson, *An Exposition of the Creed* (ed. T. Chevalier, Cambridge, 1859), 718.

[9] See the article on "Resurrection of the Dead" in the *New Catholic Encyclopedia.*

[10] See further Alois Winklhofer, *The Coming of His Kingdom: a Theology of the Last Things,* London, 1963, chapter 12, and Heinriche Heppe, *Reformed Dogmatics,* 707ff.

[11] *The Confession of Faith,* 125.

[12] *Reformed Confessions* (ed. A. Cochrane), 329-30.

[13] For further discussion see G. C. Berkouwer, *The Return of Christ,* Grand Rapids, Michigan, 1972, chapter 7.

[14] A. A. Hoekema, *The Bible and the Future,* chapter 20, 274.

[15] *Vatican Council II. The Conciliar Documents* (ed. A. Flannery, 1975), 938.

[16] *The Lausanne Covenant* (ed. John Stott, Minneapolis, 1975), 56.

[17] Book xxii, chap. 30. There are various translations of the *City of God,* e.g., that of John Healey (revised by R. V. G. Tasker) in *Everyman's Library,* that in the Modern Library (New York) and that in the Penguin Classics. The most accessible Latin text is that by J. E. C. Welldon (SPCK, 1924).

[18] Cited by John Burnaby, *Amor Dei* (London, 1938), 242.

[19] Book xxii, chap. 29.

[20] The quotations are from Burnaby, *Amor Dei* 242-45.

[21] *St Bernard On the Love of God,* translated by a religious of C.S.M.V., rpt. by S.C.M., London, 1959, as *On Loving God.*

[22] E. L. Mascall, *Grace and Glory,* London, 1975, 68-69.

[23] Sermon cccixii, 29. Cited by Mascall, 71.

[24] Enarration on Psalm 83:8. Cited by Mascall, 71.

[25] *City of God,* xix, chap. 13.

[26] Enarration on Psalm 94:33. Cited by Burnaby, *Amor Dei,* 249.

[27] Calvin, *Institutes,* Book III, chap. xxv, sec. 10.

[28] See further the article, "Beatific Vision," in the *New Catholic Encyclopedia* and the illuminating discussion by G. C. Berkouwer, *The Return of Christ,* chap. 12.

[29] The concept of the *visio dei* in the Greek and Russian Ortho- dox churches is different from that in the Roman Catholic church since the possibility of "seeing" the essence of God is denied. A distinction is made between the divine essence and the divine ener- gies, as expounded by Gregory Palamas. The Christian in heaven who participates in the energies of God is believed to be seeing God "face to face." See further Kallistos Ware, "Christian Theology in the East, 600-1453," in *A History of Christian Doctrine* (ed. H. Cunliffe-Jones with B. Drewery, Edinburgh, 1978), 181ff.

[30] Schmaus, *Justification and the Last Things,* 266.

[31] See further H. Quistorp, *Calvin's Doctrine of the Last Things,* London, 1955, 162ff.

[32] *The Works of Jonathan Edwards,* ed. Edward Hickman, Carlisle, Pa., 1974, vol. 3., 905ff.

[33] On the question, Where is heaven now? Austin Farrer has writ- ten: "According to Einstein's unanswerable reasoning, space is not an infinite pre-existent field or area in which bits of matter float about. Space is a web of intersections between material energies which form a system by thus intersecting. Unless the beings or ener- gies of which heaven is composed are of a sort to intersect physically with the energies in our physical world, heaven can be as dimen- sional as it likes, without ever getting pulled into our spatial field, or having any possible contact with us of any physical kind. There may well be contacts which are not physical at all between earthly minds and heavenly minds but that's another story." "Heaven and Hell," *Saving Belief,* London 1964, 145.

[34] A. A. Hodge, *Evangelical Theology*, 399-402, and B. H. Streeter, "The Life of the World to Come," *Immortality* (ed. B. H. Streeter, London, 1917, 154ff.

·CHAPTER·
8

Hell

Neither the Apostles' nor the Nicene Creeds mention hell or Satan. To add to either of these the words, "and in one devil, tempter and enemy of souls; and in damnation to hell everlasting," would sound odd; belief in Satan and hell is of a different nature than belief in God and heaven. The contents of the creeds point to realities which are to lay hold upon us and grip us in faith and love: Satan and hell are to be avoided, not greeted.

Belief in Satan and hell does, however, come into statements of faith made by the Church over the centuries, as well, of course, in the theological systems of teachers of doctrine and dogma. Cyprian of Carthage, writing in the third century, said:

> The damned will burn for ever in hell. Devouring flames will be their eternal portion. Their torments will never have diminution or end. Their lamentations will be vain and entreaties ineffectual. Their repentance comes too late. They will have to believe in an eternal punishment, as they refused to believe in the life eternal.[1]

And from the fifth century the *Quicunque Vult* (the so-called Athanasian Creed) has as its opening sentence these words: "Whosoever wishes to be saved, before all things it is necessary that he hold the catholic faith, which faith, if anyone does not keep it whole and unharmed, without doubt he will perish everlastingly."[2] In the next century the teaching of Origen and his disciples that the fires of hell were not everlasting and that hell had an end when all, being purged, finally entered heaven, was condemned: "He who holds that the torment of hell are temporary only and will have an end or that the damned will be re-established in the condition in which they were before they sinned, let him be anathema."[3] At the "General Council" of the Lateran in 1215, the faith was defined in these terms: "Christ will render to every man, be he damned or elect, according to his works. The damned will go into everlasting punishment with the devil, and the elect will go with Christ into glory everlasting."[4] Further, as we noted in chapter seven, the doctrine of hell as everlasting punishment is clearly stated in the Protestant Confessions of Faith of the sixteenth and seventeenth centuries. Following the Parousia, the resurrection of the dead, and the last judgment, hell will become an everlasting reality for the damned.

This traditional, orthodox doctrine of hell, common to medieval Christendom, Roman Catholicism, and Protestantism, has been challenged by two alternative doctrines. One of these interprets hell in terms of annihilation so that following the last judgment, hell lasts merely for a "short time" before it and its members become as nothing. The other, known as *apocatastasis* (as taught by Origen), is the teaching that all free, moral creatures—angels, human beings, and demons—will ultimately be saved, even perhaps after a period of purging in hell. Thus hell is only temporary in comparison with heaven, which is truly everlasting. We shall return to Origen in the next chapter when we discuss universalism. Our task in this chapter is to examine the doctrine of hell as everlasting punishment and then to look at the doctrine of hell as annihilation. In each case we shall be particularly interested in the way Scripture is used and interpreted.

Everlasting punishment

Medieval theologians distinguished between *poena damni* (the pain of loss), interpreted in terms of the loss of the *visio dei*, and the *poena sensus* (the pain of sense), interpreted in terms of suffering. This passed over into both Roman Catholic and Protestant theology and was developed in various ways.[5] Calvin dealt with the lot of the reprobate in the last section of book three of the *Institutes*, as well as at appropriate places in his biblical commentaries. He wrote:[6]

> Now because no description can deal adequately with the gravity of God's vengeance against the wicked, their torments and tortures are figuratively expressed to us by physical things, that is by darkness, weeping and gnashing of teeth (Matt. 8:12; 22:13), unquenchable fire (Matt. 3:12; Mark 9:43; Isa. 66:24), and undying worm gnawing at the heart (Isa. 66:24). By such expressions the Holy Spirit certainly intended to confound all our senses with dread. . . . As by such details we should be enabled in some degree to conceive the lot of the wicked, so we ought especially to fix our thoughts upon this: how wretched it is to be cut off from all fellowship with God. And not that only, but so to feel his sovereign power against you that you cannot escape being pressed by it. For first, his displeasure is like a raging fire, devouring and engulfing everything it touches. Secondly, all creatures so serve him in the execution of his judgment that they to whom the Lord will openly show his wrath will feel heaven, earth, sea, living beings and all that exists aflame, as it were, with dire anger against them and armed to destroy them.

Here we have both the pain of loss and the pain of sense imposed directly by God in his wrath.

The Genevan reformer was certainly not a literalist in his interpretation of the fire of hell. Commenting upon Matthew 3:12 and recalling medieval theological speculation he wrote:

Many persons, I am aware, have entered into ingenious debates about the eternal fire by which the wicked will be tormented after the judgment. But we may conclude from many passages of Scripture, that it is a metaphorical expression. For, if we must believe that it is real, or what they call material fire, we must also believe that the brimstone and the fan are material, both of them being mentioned in Isaiah (30:33). We must explain the fire in the same manner as the worm (Mark 8:44,46,48) and, if it is universally agreed that the worm is a metaphorical term, we must form the same opinion as to the fire. Let us lay aside the speculations, by which foolish men weary themselves to no purpose, and satisfy ourselves with believing, that these forms of speech denote in a manner suited to our feeble capacity, a dreadful torment, which no man can now comprehend, and no language can express.[7]

As the founder of the Jesuits and a leader of the Roman Catholic counter-reformation, Ignatius Loyola (d.1556) is justly famous. He had a vivid belief in the existence of hell and expected his religious order to share it. This is revealed in his *The Spiritual Exercises*, a series of meditations and rules designed to lead people to conquer their passions and give themselves wholly to God.[8] Beginning with systematic consideration of sin and its consequences, the book culminates in meditations upon the risen, glorified Lord. The fifth exercise in the book is a meditation on hell:

The first part will be to see with the eye of the imagination those great fires, and those souls as it were in bodies of fire. The second to hear with the ears lamentations, howlings, cries, blasphemies against Christ our Lord and against all his saints. The third, with the sense of smell, to smell smoke, brimstone, refuse and rottenness. The fourth, to taste with the taste bitter things, as tears, sadness and the worm of conscience. The fifth, to feel with the sense of touch how those fires do touch and burn souls.

It would seem that Ignatius was much nearer to the literal rather than the metaphorical sense in his interpretation of the biblical texts: As such he was in line with most of the medieval writers who believed that the fires of hell had a physical or material character to them since they were directed toward resurrected bodies (which, though incorruptible, could still feel the pain of fire.)[9]

We turn next to the Church of England and the classic exposition of the Apostles' Creed by Bishop Pearson (1659), which we quoted in the last chapter. After providing arguments against the Socinian doctrine of hell as annihilation, he summarized his explanation of hell in these words:[10]

> That the wicked after this life shall be punished for their sins, so that in their punishment there shall be a demonstration of the justice of God revealed against all unrighteousness of men. That to this end they shall be raised again to life, and shall be judged and condemned by Christ, and delivered up under the curse, to be tormented with the devil and his angels. That the punishment which shall be inflicted on them shall be proportionate to their sins, as a recompense of their demerits, so that no man shall suffer more than he hath deserved. That they shall be tormented with a pain of loss, the loss from God, from whose presence they are cast out, the pain from themselves, in despair of enjoying him, and regret for losing him. That they farther shall be tormented with the pain of sense inflicted on them by the wrath of God which abideth upon them, represented unto us by a lake of fire. That their persons shall continue for ever in this remediless condition, under an everlasting pain of sense, because there is no hope of heaven, under an eternal pain of sense, because there is no means to appease the wrath of God which abideth on them.

This is the classic doctrine, but without the commitment to the view that the fire and smoke are to be taken in the literal sense.

Not only in the teaching of its divines but also within its Prayer Book does the Church of England set forth the doctrine of hell as everlasting punishment. In the *Book of Common Prayer* (in the 1549, 1552 and definitive 1662 editions) there is a service to be used on the first day of Lent called *A Commination, or Denouncing of God's Anger and Judgements against Sinners.* This is based on a similar service used in the medieval Church. Commination is from *comminari* meaning "to threaten," and the whole service is around this theme, containing God's cursing of sinners and his threat that the unrepentant shall go to hell. Here is part of the long address read by the minister:

> The day of the Lord cometh as a thief in the night: and when men shall say, "Peace," and all things are safe, then shall sudden destruction come upon them. . . . Then shall appear the wrath of God in the day of vengeance, which obstinate sinners, through the stubborness of their heart, have heaped upon themselves. . . . O terrible voice of most just judgment, which shall be pronounced upon them, when it shall be said unto them, "Go, ye cursed, into the fire everlasting, which is prepared for the devil and his angels." Therefore, brethren, take we heed betime, while the day of salvation lasteth; for the night cometh, when none can work. But let us, while we have the light, believe in the light; that we be not cast into utter darkness, where is weeping and gnashing of teeth.

In keeping with the general decline in belief in hell, this service does not appear in the modern Anglican Prayer Books. Those who read it cannot avoid the conclusion that it certainly teaches both the *poena damni* and *poena sensus.*[11]

One man who was familiar with this service of commination was that best known of English Puritans, Richard Baxter (1615-1691). Among his many writings is found his classic, *The Saints' Everlasting Rest: a treatise of the blessed state of the saints in their enjoyment of God in heaven* (1650), which is both doctrinal and practical theology. It is an extended exposition of Hebrews 4:9, "There remaineth therefore a rest to the people of God." Within its pages Baxter also describes hell in order to persuade his readers to long for heaven and prepare diligently to go there.[12] In a chapter on "the misery of those who lose the Saints' Rest" he describes what a person loses by not being reconciled to God in Christ Jesus. In their loss of heaven the ungodly (1) lose the glorious, personal perfection which the saints enjoy in heaven—"that shining lustre of the body surpassing the brightness of the sun at noon-day"; (2) they shall have no comfortable relation to God nor communion with him—"God will abhor to retain them in his household"; (3) they lose all delightful affections towards God—"God suits men's employment to their natures"; and (4) they shall be deprived of the blessed society of angels and glorified saints—"they must be members of the corporation of hell."

This loss of heaven will be most tormenting because their understandings will be cleared to know their loss, their consciences will make them fully aware of their guilt, and their affections will no longer be stupified. The memory of their past lives and how they offended God will ever be before them and they will fully recognize the enormity of their sin. These torments will be the greater because of the actual sufferings of hell. Baxter insists that "the principal author of hell-torments is God himself," and "his wrath will be an intolerable burden to their souls." Both the place and the state of this torment are "purposely ordained to glorify the justice of God." Thus "the everlasting flames of hell will not be thought too hot for the rebellious; and when they have there burned through millions of ages, he will not repent them of the evil which is befallen them." In fact, the "torments of the damned must be extreme because they are the effect of divine vengeance." Certainly "God had rather men would accept of

Christ and mercy, yet when they persist in their rebellion, he will take pleasure in their execution"; thus "woe to the souls whom God rejoiceth to punish!" And the punishment will be felt by both body and soul, but chiefly the soul. The torments will be without mitigation and "when a thousand million of ages are past they will be as fresh to begin as the first day." Thus "as the joys of heaven are beyond our conception, so are the pains of hell. Everlasting torment is inconceivable torment."

Baxter believed it was necessary to speak about hell in order to make people aware of their destiny and cause them to repent of their sin and turn to Christ as Savior. Jonathan Edwards, who lived a century after Baxter and in a different continent, also shared this conviction and has left us many sermons of this kind. Obviously Edwards was a man who often thought about both heaven and hell and then wrote and preached on these awesome topics. His doctrine is that of Reformed theology and traditional orthodoxy, but his treatment of hell is rightly specially noticed because of its intensity, vividness, and comprehensiveness. He appears to have thought about every aspect and, in his published writings as well as unpublished manuscripts, to have given abundant evidence of this profound thinking and lively imagination.[13]

John Gerstner offers this summary of Edwards' doctrine of hell:

Hell is a spiritual and material furnace of fire where its victims are exquisitely tortured in their minds and in their bodies eternally, according to their various capacities, by God, the devils and damned humans including themselves, in their memories and consciences, as well as in their raging unsatisfied lusts, from which place of death God's saving grace, mercy and pity are gone forever, never for a moment to return.[14]

Unlike Calvin, and in a more obvious way than Baxter, Edwards believed that the fires of hell were both physical and figurative (metaphorical). This is clear in many of his sermons, but it also comes out clearly in his description of hell in his great treatise, *A History of the Work of Redemption* (1774). In Part IX on "The General Judgment" he describes the Parousia, resurrection, and judgment. Then he relates how Christ would ascend again from this earth a second time, taking his mystical body, the whole Church, with him into heaven. Here is his description of hell:[15]

> When they are gone, this world shall be set on fire, and be turned into a great furnace, wherein all the enemies of Christ and his church shall be tormented for ever and ever. This is manifest by 2 Peter 3:7. . . . When Christ and his church are ascended to a distance from this world—that miserable company of the wicked being left behind, to have their sentence executed upon them here—then this whole lower world shall be set on fire, either from heaven, or by fire breaking out of the bowels of the earth, or both, as it was with the water in the time of the deluge. However, this lower world shall be set all on fire. How will it strike the wicked with horror, when the fire begins to lay hold upon them and they find no way to escape from it! What shrieking and crying will there be among those many millions, when they begin to enter into this great furnace, when the whole world shall be a furnace of the fiercest and most raging heat. . . .
>
> And here shall all the persecutors of the church of God burn in everlasting fire, who had before burnt the saints at the stake; and shall suffer torments far beyond all that their utmost wit and malice could inflict on the saints. And here the bodies of all the wicked shall burn and be tormented to all eternity, and never be consumed; and the wrath of God shall be poured out on their souls. . . . And now, the devil, that old serpent, shall receive his full punishment. . . . This world, which formerly used to be the place of his kingdom, where he set up himself as God, shall now be the place of his complete punishment, of full and everlasting torment.

And in common with other theologians, Edwards pictured the saints in heaven being able to "look down" and magnify the justice of God in the punishment of the ungodly. But, differing from other theologians who looked for the total renewal of the cosmos to become the "new heavens and new earth," Edwards placed heaven "above" and saw hell as the continuation of this cosmos but as engulfed in eternal fire.

In the century after Edward's died, belief in hell as everlasting evil and punishment declined within the Church. Nevertheless it was still taught by conservative Roman Catholics, Protestants, and Anglican Anglo-Catholics. The leader of the latter for many years in the nineteenth century was Professor E. B. Pusey of Oxford, and in 1879-80, as an old man, he arose to defend the doctrine of everlasting punishment in hell at a time when senior churchmen were either questioning it or denying it.[16] Unlike the Reformed theologians we have been quoting, Pusey had an "Arminian" (better, Greek Orthodox) view of human free will. In his book, *What is of Faith as to Everlasting Punishment* (1880), he set out his position in this way:[17]

1. Without freewill, man would be inferior to the lower animals, which have a sort of limited freedom of choice.

2. Absolute freewill implies the power of choosing amiss and, having chosen amiss, to persevere in choosing amiss. It would be self-contradictory that Almighty God should create a free agent capable of loving Him, without being capable also of rejecting His love.

3. The higher and more complete and pervading the freewill is, the more completely an evil choice will pervade and disorder the whole being.

4. But without freewill we could not freely love God. Freedom is a condition of love.

5. In eternity those who behold Him will know what the bliss is, eternally to love Him. But then that bliss involves the intolerable misery of losing Him through our own evil choice. To lose God and be alienated from Him is in itself Hell, or the vestibule of Hell.

6. But that His creatures may not lose Him, God, when He

created all His rational creatures with freewill, created them also in grace, so that they had the full power to choose aright, and could not choose amiss, except by resisting the drawing of God to love Him.

7. The only hindrance to man's salvation is, in any case, the obstinate misuse of that freewill, with which God endowed him, in order that he might freely love Him.

8. God wills that all should be saved, if they *will* it, and to this end gave His Son to die for them, and the Holy Ghost to teach them.

9. The merits of Jesus reach to every soul who wills to be saved, whether in this life they knew Him or knew Him not.

10. God the Holy Ghost visits every soul which God has created, and each soul will be judged as it responded or did not respond to the degree of light which He bestowed on it, not by our maxims, but by the wisdom and love of Almighty God.

11. We know absolutely nothing of the proportion of the saved to the lost, or who will be lost; but this we *do* know, that none will be lost, who do not obstinately to the end and in the end refuse God. None will be lost, whom God *can* save, without destroying in them His own gift of freewill.

12. With regard to the *nature* of the sufferings, nothing is matter of faith. No one doubts that the very special suffering will be the loss of God (poena damni): that, being what they are, they know that they were made by God for Himself, and yet, through their own obstinate will, will not have Him. As to 'pains of sense' the Church has nowhere laid down as a matter of faith, the material character of the worm and the fire, or that they denote more than the gnawing of remorse. Although then it would be very rash to lay down dogmatically, that the 'fire' is *not* to be understood literally, as it has been understood almost universally by Christians; yet no one has a right to urge those representations, from which the imagination so shrinks, as a ground for refusing to believe in Hell, since he is left free not to believe them.

Thus, unlike Calvin, Pusey teaches a doctrine of hell as everlasting punishment which is tied to a strongly asserted doctrine of the freedom of the will to accept or reject grace and to a view of predestination more like that of Arminius and John Wesley than that of Augustine.

A century after Pusey published his book, it is difficult to find leading Protestant churchmen or theologians who actually believe in hell as everlasting punishment and who are prepared to state that belief in either sermons or books. Here and there a biblical scholar will express this belief. For example, C. Ryder Smith, an English Methodist, wrote: "To the present writer it seems impossible, if the evidence is considered objectively, to deny that there is a doctrine of everlasting punishment in the New Testament."[18] And some theologians insist on the possibility of hell but refrain from further definitive comments.[19] Even in conservative circles there is a seeming reluctance to espouse publicly a doctrine of hell, and where it is held there is a seeming tendency towards a doctrine of hell as annihilation.[20]

Within Roman Catholicism there is still the adherence to the traditional doctrine, especially from the conservative elements within the Vatican. In 1979 the Sacred Congregation for the Doctrine of the Faith published a document entitled "The Reality of Life after Death." In this it is written:

> In fidelity to the New Testament and Tradition, the Church believes in the happiness of the just who will one day be with Christ. She believes that there will be eternal punishment for the sinner, who will be deprived of the sight of God, and that this punishment will have repercussion on the whole being of the sinner.[12]

In his treatment of eschatology (at which we have already looked) Schmaus is reluctant to say that there will be no hell, for he believes it remains as a possibility. He calls it a scandal and suggests that "there is no community of the damned;

every lost soul exists in such frigid isolation that he is not even aware of whether there are other souls in hell."[22] And Schmaus's hesitation to speak of hell in objective terms is found in greater measure in other Roman Catholic theologians such as Karl Rahner and Hans Küng.[23] There are, however, some Roman Catholic writers, less well known than the ones to whom we have made reference, who do teach a traditional doctrine of hell. One is Josef Staudinger, S. J., *Life Hereafter* (1964), whose description of the fires of hell and everlasting punishment and torment is very much that of the older Roman Catholic text books. Another is Alois Winklhofer, *The Coming of His Kingdom: a theology of the last things* (1963); though this writer is a biblical exegete and not a dogmatic theologian, he still follows orthodox doctrine in his exposition of hell.

Annihilation

The teaching that the soul and body (i.e., the whole person) ceases to exist at death and will never again exist is certainly held by many people in the West, but it is not a Christian doctrine. In theological talk the word annihilation is used in two ways. First of all, it is tied to the doctrine of conditional immortality and the sleep of the soul between death and the general resurrection of the dead; the bodies of the wicked are raised at the last day and, after judgment, punished before passing into oblivion and nothingness. In contrast the bodies of the righteous live for ever in the glory of the kingdom of God. We shall call this approach "conditional immortality." Second, it is used to describe the fate of those who, though possessing immortal souls, are nevertheless caused to fall into non-existence after a period in hell; this approach, which accepts the reality of hell but presumes that it is not eternal in the same sense as heaven is eternal, is best given the description of "annihilationism." Needless to say these two views are often confused and any form of annihilation is often assumed to be based upon conditional immortality. In fact annihilationism proper, as it is suggested in the writings of recent Anglican divines, appears to be a way of mitigating and lessening the reality of hell which, in the opinion of these theologians, is too strongly embedded in Scripture and Tradition to be ignored or denied. Thus it is based more on the assumed character of God and ideas of punishment than upon detailed biblical exegesis, which is the method normally used by those who teach conditional immortality.[24]

Our interest here is with conditional immortality, which appears to be gaining acceptance in evangelical orthodox circles. There is a fine exposition of different types of the doctrine of conditional immortality by J. H. Leckie in his *The World to Come and Final Destiny* (1918); in fact he finds four kinds—that related to evolutionary theory, that based upon philosophical reasoning, that which tends, in varing degrees of definiteness, to move towards the full doctrine, and the biblical, theological, systematic form. He judges that Edward White's *Life in Christ* (revised and expanded edition, 1878) was the most important exposition from a biblical standpoint; it was widely read. Geoffrey Rowell's *Hell and the Victorians* (1974) offers invaluable information and comment on the controversies surrounding conditional immortality. Finally, the vast work of L. E. Froom on behalf of the Seventh-Day Adventists brings together whatever evidence there is that conditional immortality is a respectable doctrine to hold; it is titled, *The Conditionalist Faith of our Fathers* (2 vols. and 2476 pages of useful but often undigested information, 1965-66).

Rather than looking at the tedious contents of the debates of the past, we will look briefly at the arguments for conditional immortality produced by a leading English evangelical scholar. Basil F. C. Atkinson was an Under-Librarian in the

University Library, Cambridge, from 1925 to 1960. He became renowned in evangelical circles, not least in Cambridge, for his gifts as a leader of devotional Bible readings. He
released in the late 1960s a private publication titled, *Life and
Immortality: An Examination of the Nature and Meaning of Life
and Death as they are revealed in the Scriptures*. Atkinson used
all his linguistic gifts to argue that the Bible clearly teaches
(1) unconscious existence from death to the general resurrection; (2) the eternal joy of the redeemed in their glorious resurrection bodies from the resurrection and for ever, and (3)
the annihilation of the ungodly after they have been raised to
appear before the throne of judgment and suitably punished
there. And, he insisted, the Bible does not teach the doctrine
of the immortality of the soul.

Atkinson's arguments for the annihilation of the person after the last judgment are based wholly on biblical exegesis: He
refuses to use any arguments based upon the character of God
and upon ideas of what is just or unjust punishment. In the
chapter titled, "The Doom of the Lost," he goes to great
lengths to seek to prove that all the key words traditionally
used to point to an everlasting punishment are better understood as pointing to a punishment that is everlasting in its
effects—that is, they mean extinction, nothingness, annihilation. In fact, because he has such a high view of the inspiration and authority of the Bible, this is the only way he can
proceed. He accepts all the "severe" sayings of Jesus and his
apostles/evangelists and attempts to prove that they have
been wrongly interpreted by the majority of theologians because they allowed the doctrine of the immortality of the soul
to affect their reading of the words in the sacred text.

To follow the arguments of Atkinson would prove tedious.
Suffice it to note that, as illustrative of his reasoning, he interpreted Matthew 25:46 and 2 Thessalonians 1:9 in this manner. On "everlasting punishment" (Matt. 25:46) he
commented:

Many have relied on this phrase to support the idea of the ever-lasting conscious suffering of the wicked, reading it as if it said, "everlasting punishing". This is not the meaning of the word. When the adjective *aionios* meaning "everlasting" is used in Greek with nouns of *action*, it has reference to the *result* of that action, not the process. Thus the phrase "everlasting punishment" is comparable to "everlasting redemption" and "everlasting salvation", both scriptural phrases. No one supposes that we are being redeemed or being saved for ever. We were redeemed and saved once for all by Christ with eternal results. In the same way the lost will not be passing through a process of punishment for ever but will be punished once and for all with eternal results.

On "everlasting destruction from the presence of the Lord" (2 Thess. 1:9), he claims that this points to total exclusion from the presence of God and that this exclusion is personal extinction and annihilation.

Nowhere does Atkinson refer to the Jewish apocalyptic sources and their teaching on the doom of the lost. Two scholars who do refer to these sources and who tentatively come to similar conclusions to Atkinson are William Strawson, *Jesus and the Future Life* (1959) and J. Arthur Baird, *The Justice of God in the Teaching of Jesus* (1963).[25] However, neither Strawson nor Baird would have called themselves conservative evangelicals in the sense that Atkinson so called himself. Further, it is not clear whether these two writers actually commit themselves to such doctrines as the sleep of the soul.

Stephen H. Travis, a conservative evangelical writer, claims "that it is difficult to decide between annihilation and eternal torment on purely exegetical grounds" since terms like 'Gehenna' and 'destruction' are not precise enough for a clear-cut decision." The New Testament writers deal largely in images rather than in precise theological definition, and the issue of eternal torment or annihilation was not in the minds of those who wrote the New Testament.

The most significant thing about the destiny of unbelievers is that they will be separated from Christ. Compared with this tragic fact, there is little point in asking whether the lost continue to be conscious or are annihilated. It is because later Christians have been more concerned about happiness and misery than about relationship to God that they have persisted in asking such questions.[26]

Another respected conservative writer, John Wenham, who knew Basil Atkinson and finds himself attracted to Atkinson's conclusions, nevertheless is aware that the pursuit of the doctrine of conditional immortality by evangelicals may be a dangerous cul-de-sac. He offers five caveats to those who might be tempted to abandon the traditional view too easily:[27]

1. Beware of the immense natural appeal of any way out that evades the idea of everlasting sin and suffering. The temptation to twist what may be quite plain statements of Scripture is intense. It is the ideal situation for unconscious rationalizing.

2. Beware of the pervasive and insidious influence of the present liberal *Zeitgeist* on all our thinking. . . . Such a doctrine as unending torment would inevitably be a natural point for merciless attack in a climate of opinion committed to the elimination of everything offensive to modern sentiment.

3. Note that the modern revival of conditionalism was pioneered mainly by Socinians and Arians, who rejected such fundamental doctrines as the deity of Christ, and that today it constitutes an important element in the teaching of Jehovah's Witnesses and Christadelphians. Be wary of such bedfellows.[28]

4. Note that the adoption of conditionalism, even if it can be accepted as a possible interpretation of the Bible, does not solve all the difficulties. It can never be easy to accept the idea that God will decree the annihilation of beings made in

his own image, nor that he will decree pain that will be of no benefit to the sufferer. . . .

5. Beware of weakening zeal for the gospel. The gospel should be preached with passionate urgency. One who has believed that the alternative to faith in Christ is unending misery in hell may well find that the sudden loss of confidence in the doctrine will leave him deflated, with the edge of his evangelistic zeal impaired.

Let us hope that he will be heard and this matter seriously and reverently discussed by theologians and pastors.

Notes

[1] Cyprian, *Ad Demetrianum*, c. 24, cited by J. Staudinger, *Life Hereafter*, 211.

[2] The "Athanasian Creed" is printed in the Anglican *Book of Common Prayer (1662)*; for a study of it see J. N. D. Kelly, *The Athanasian Creed*, London, 1964.

[3] For the text of the nine anathemas of the Emperor Justinian against Origen see *Nicene and Post-Nicene Fathers, Second Series, Vol. 14, The Seven Ecumenical Councils*, Edinburgh, 1900, rpt. Grand Rapids, 1977, 320.
ument 429.

[5] See for example H. Heppe, *Reformed Dogmatics*, 711-12.

[6] *Institutes*, III, xxv, 12.

[7] Calvin, *Commentary on a Harmony of the Evangelists*, Grand Rapids, 1949, vol. 1, 200.

[8] There are English translations of the *Spiritual Exercises* by W. H. Longridge (London 1919) and T. Corbishley, S. J. (London, 1963).

[9] This material fire is taught not only by the academic theologians but also it is presupposed in Dante's *Inferno* and in Michaelangelo's awe-inspiring painting of the last judgment and the fall of the damned into hell, in the Sistine Chapel, Rome.

[10] Pearson, *An Exposition of the Creed*, 728.

[11] In the *Litany or General Supplication*, which is also part of the *Book of Common Prayer*, there is the request, "From thy wrath and from everlasting damnation, Good Lord deliver us."

[12] Baxter's treatise has been reprinted in its full form as well as in various abridged forms. I have used the 1928 London edition introduced by M. Monckton. This has two chapters on the theme of hell, chaps. V and VI.

[13] See further John H. Gerstener, *Jonathan Edwards on Heaven and Hell*, Grand Rapids, 1980.

[14] Ibid., 53.

[15] Edwards, *Works*, vol. 1, 614.

[16] For the context of his book see G. Rowell, *Hell and the Victorians*, chap. 7.

[17] Pusey, *What is of Faith*, 22-23. This is reprinted in H. P. Liddon, *Life of E. B. Pusey*, London, 1898, vol. 4, 350-351, where also is a collection of letters on the same topic.

[18] C. Ryder Smith, *The Bible Doctrine of the Hereafter*, 220.

[19] These include G. C. Berkouwer, Emil Brunner, and Karl Rahner.

[20] This assertion is difficult to prove, but it is based on the writer's conversations over a number of years with evangelical theologians.

[21] Printed in *Vatican II: More Postconciliar Documents* (ed. A. Flannery, Grand Rapids, 1982), vol. 2, 502.

[22] Schmaus, *Justification and the Last Things*, 253ff.

[23] See the discussion of Roman Catholic theology by B. Hebblethwaite, *The Christian Hope*, 153ff.

[24] E.g., O. C. Quick, *Doctrines of the Creed*, London, 1938, 257ff., U. Simon, *The End Is Not Yet*, London, 1964, and W. Temple, *Christus Veritas*, London 1924. It is also suggested in the *Commentary on Revelation* by G. B. Caird, to which reference was made in chapter five.

[25] Strawson, 154-55, and Baird, 233-36.

[26] Stephen H. Travis, *Christian Hope and the Future of Man*, 135-136.

[27] John W. Wenham, *The Goodness of God*, 37-39.

[28] Here Mr. Wenham confuses conditional immortality and annihilationism, as we have defined them. The Socinians taught a form of annihilationism while various modern sects teach a form of conditional immortality which includes the idea of the annihilation of the wicked. See further A. A. Hoekema, *The Bible and the Future*, 266, as well as his *Four Major Cults*.

· CHAPTER ·
9

Universalism

The general decline in belief in an everlasting hell has not only contributed to the increasing use of the word "hell" to describe conditions on earth (as in "the *hell* of Stalingrad" and "the *hell* of Dachau") but has also been accompanied within the churches by the assumption that most, if not all, humanity will get to heaven. Universalism is the word normally used by theologians to describe the doctrine that ultimately and finally all humanity without exception will enter into the everlasting life. Another way of expressing it is to say that it is the doctrine that since no soul can have been created for final condemnation no soul can in the end be lost. Not all those who would call themselves (or be called by others) universalists necessarily suppose that there will be no hell (for there may be a "temporary" hell for some) or that the total number in heaven will be equivalent to the total number of human beings and angels originally created (for some angels and humans may be annihilated). What universalism does require is that finally from everlasting to everlasting there be no person left in hell or not included in the kingdom of heaven.

The word *Apokatastis* is sometimes used as the equivalent of universalism. It is found only once in the New Testament, in Acts 3:21 (a verse that describes the Parousia of Christ and the consummation of God's purposes), and is translated by such words as "restitution," "establishing," and "restoration." In fact the expression *apokatastasis pantōn* in this verse does not mean the conversion of all humankind but the restoration of all things and circumstances which the prophets of the Old Testament had predicted, including the renewal of the earth. Thus the use of the word by Origen and many after him to point to universal salvation is not a happy one.

Universalism comes in a variety of forms from the sophisticated to the sentimental and in ancient and modern dress. Arguments for it change, but it seems to have a constant attraction for the religious mind. We shall briefly look at some of these types of universalism and then conclude with some remarks on the universal nature of the gospel.

Universalism via hell

From the third to the fifth centuries a Platonic form of Christian universalism lurked in the theological shadows, ready to be seen in the full light of day and be adopted as church teaching. Augustine's remarks concerning this possibility and the seriousness with which he treats the topic in his *City of God* reveal how widespread was universalism in the early fifth century.[1] The most important advocate of universalism was Origen of Alexandria (ca. 185-254); see his *On First Principles*, Book 2, chapters 1-3, and Book 3, chapters 5-6.[2] He taught that ultimately all free, moral creatures—angels, devils and human beings—will share in the grace of salvation. He built his great system of cosmic evolution on two principles—the freedom of the will and the goodness of God. According to his Platonic philosophy he understood this world as part of a great cycle of the emanation of all things from God and the return of all things to God.

God created rational spirits and souls in order that they might contemplate his perfection; but with the exception of a few of the very highest of the angels (rational spirits) and the human soul of Christ, all the rest of the rational creatures declined to some extent their life of pure contemplation and fell away from God. Those who fell the least we know as angels; those that fell the farthest we know as devils, and in between are what we call human beings, eternal souls in bodies of flesh and blood. Thus human bodies are a punishment for falling away from God. Souls were once "minds" but lost their purely intellectual character in the process of falling away from God. (Origen's teaching on the pre-existence of the soul was later condemned as heresy.) The world is God's provision for fallen creatures. Here, with genuine freedom of the will, human beings begin the long ascent back to God, the heavenly Father, who gently coaxes them home. Likewise even the devils are coaxed back to God in the same process which goes on for souls after life in this world.

Hell for Origen was a different place/sphere from that envisaged by his contemporary, Tertullian, who in his treatise, *On Spectacles*, portrays heaven's great feature as the superb view of the damned frying in hell. For Origen all punishments are remedial; thus he interpreted the fires of hell as purifying experiences, including torments of conscience, and the outer darkness he saw as deep ignorance of spiritual reality. Not only the baptized but all people are involved in the cosmic process of sanctification so that at the end they with all purified rational spirits will return to their original condition—the pure and holy contemplation of God. Then God shall be all in all.

The doctrine of the final restoration of all souls to God was taught by Gregory of Nyssa (but without much of Origen's Platonism) and is attributed to Diodore of Tarsus and Theodore of Mopsuestia, while Gregory of Nazianzus believed it was an open question.[3] Though a package of Origenist doctrines (e.g., pre-existence of the soul and *apokatastis*) was condemned at a council in Constantinople in 543, there is some doubt whether the condemnation of universalism as such was repeated by the Fifth Ecumenical Council held in Constantinople in 553.[4] Other teachers of universalism influenced by Platonic philosophy include John Scotus Erigena in the ninth century and Peter Sterry and Jeremiah White in the seventeenth century.[5]

Origen was wedded not only to a Platonic philosophy but also to allegorical interpretation of the Bible, which allowed him to reject the literal sense in favor of that meaning he wanted to establish through allegorical interpretation.[6]

Universalism via annihilation

Already we have referred to this position, espoused this century by leading Anglican writers. Most recently Brian Hebblethwaite has written:[7]

If creatures can rebel against the divine ground of their being to such an extent as to render themselves absolutely unredeemable then there seems no point in God's keeping them in being for ever in such an unending state of deprivation. It is much more plausible to suppose that the language of damnation and everlasting loss is symbolic language, designed to bring out the awesome possibility that a man may by his actions and his attitudes forfeit his eternal destiny and render himself incapable of being drawn into the love and life of God. But if such a terrible possibility is fulfilled, it must mean that the lost one brings about his own annihilation and disappears from being rather than that he is raised for ever and held in a state of everlasting damnation. The sheer pointlessness of such a state being allowed to continue for ever shows clearly that conditional immortality is more religiously and morally plausible than everlasting punishment.

But he really does not want to believe in annihilation, for he continues:

One would like to be able to hope that even the possibility of eternal loss in the sense of annihilation is never in fact realised. To suppose that there comes a time when the God of love, who went to the lengths of the Cross of Christ to win men's love in return, has to write off a created person as absolutely unredeemable is a hard supposition for a Christian to make.

In fact he wants to believe in a second chance after death in a process which is like a purgatory for all (baptized and unbaptized alike). He says:

> Once we free ourselves from the old idea that opportunities to repent and respond to God's love are restricted to a single lifespan on earth, we may be the readier to hope that God's patient, self-sacrificial love will in the end prevail over even the most recalcitrant sinner. In other words, the notion of conditional immortality makes greater sense in conjunction with the old idea of the finality of death. In the context of an extended "purgatorial" phase of experience and growth beyond death, it makes greater sense at least to hope that universalism may be true.

Thus his position is universalism perhaps via annihilation but more probably without annihilation. We add that when a "second chance" doctrine is proposed in the period of "probation" after death, it is often accompanied by prayers for the dead, which, unlike the traditional prayers for the souls in purgatory en route for heaven, actually request salvation for those who have died without being professing Christians. The vague and open-ended rubrics of some modern Anglican liturgies can be used in this way.[8]

Universalism decreed by God

F. D. E. Schleiermacher (1768-1834) is often called the father of modern theology.[9] He explained and expounded

Christianity as the highest historical embodiment and transmitter of God-consciousness (an immediate sense of absolute dependence). His argument for personal immortality is not based on philosophical arguments but rather on the experience of redemption and of increase of God-consciousness which Christ makes possible; this experience leads to the accepting of Christ's own conviction that man's personality survives death. Though little of a factual kind can be known about life after death and the consummation of all things, Schleiermacher did believe it right to develop what he called "prophetic doctrines concerning the last things." Thus he briefly comments on the second coming, the resurrection, the last judgment, and the *visio dei* in his *The Christian Faith*.

In this book he also explains that there is only one divine decree according to which "the totality of the new creation is called into being out of the general mass of the human race." However, he assumed that "the totality of the new creation is equal to the general mass," which is another way of saying that God has decreed the universal restoration of all souls.[10] Among his reasons for holding such a doctrine were his conviction that Christ, having assumed human nature, is truly a universal Savior and that what he came to save is a unity, the one human race. Another one was that there could not be genuine blessedness in heaven if the redeemed there knew of the pains and sufferings of friends in hell; thus for there to be true happiness in heaven there could not be a hell. Schleiermacher was of course very much aware of the presentation by many writers of a heaven which included a righteous joy in seeing the wicked justly punished for their sins against almighty God.[11] He rejected all this and insisted that human sympathy is real and cannot be avoided even when those suffering actually deserve what they are receiving. Thus there cannot be any form of hell, for if there is, then there cannot be a real, blessed heaven.

Since Schleiermacher is vague as to the "intermediate

state," it is not clear as to how and where he envisaged the totality of the human race being fully and finally drawn into eternal blessedness. Apparently few adopted Schleiermacher's scheme of universal salvation by the divine decree, but the very fact that such a famous theologian had taught it helped to make the acceptance of universalism easier by those who wanted to express it in a way different from Schleiermacher. The nineteenth century is the period when universalism gained increasing support within the main-line Protestant denominations, so that in the twentieth century it is hardly seen as a heresy, except in the distinctly evangelical and conservative churches.

Universalism as an optimistic hope

In 1914 H. R. Mackintosh wrote:

> If at this moment a frank and confidential plebiscite of the English-speaking ministry were taken, the likelihood is that a considerable majority would adhere to Universalism. They may no doubt shrink from it as a dogma, but they would cherish it privately as a hope.[12]

And four years later J. H. Leckie attempted to summarize what he called "Christian optimism" in these words:[13]

> Christian optimism finds its doctrine of the End to be justified from many points of view. When we think of the *Divine character*, we see that it is love; and infinite love has an infinite power to save and to reconcile. When we consider the *freedom of the human will*, we see that it is limited by the nature of things, by the moral necessity that good should prove itself stronger than evil. When we reflect on the *nature of evil*, we see that it is transitory, carries in it the seeds of its own destruction, has no place among immortal things. Finally, when we think of God as *having a pur-*

pose, we see that this purpose is universal, and must in the end prevail.

He had found this type of theology expressed both systematically in certain books and assumed or hinted in many other books.[14] In fact his summary is not very different from that which is heard expressed in many places, especially seminaries and colleges, today. And when other religions are being discussed, positions such as this are commonly expressed, often of course along with various theories about the relationship of these religions to Jesus Christ.[15]

Most advocates of universalism in the period before 1914 felt it right and necessary to make use of biblical texts (e.g., those predicting the salvation of all—John 12:32; Acts 3:21; Rom. 5:18; those declaring God's universalist intention—1 Tim. 2:4; 2 Pet. 3:9; and those referring to objective reconciliation—2 Cor. 5:19; Tit. 2:11; Col. 1:20; Heb. 2:9; 1 John 2:2) as the foundation of their hope and to prove that texts which appeared to suggest eternal damnation did not contain that strong doctrine. In the twentieth century there has been an increasing recognition that Jesus did actually speak of hell and that there is a doctrine of eternal damnation in the New Testament; however, this teaching has been rejected on various grounds—e.g., it came from Jewish apocalyptic sources and was not authentic Christian teaching, that the higher doctrines (i.e., the supposed universalist ones) are to be followed rather than the lower doctrines (i.e., based on Jewish apocalyptic) and that the spirit of the teaching of Jesus and his apostles is to be followed in preference to the letter of that teaching.

This latter argument was forcibly made by C. W. Emmet in an important essay entitled, "The Bible and Hell," published in 1917.[16] Emmet was an expert in Jewish apocalyptic literature and made no attempt to deny that Jesus actually used apocalyptic imagery and adopted apocalyptic doctrines. He

argued that modern teaching about the afterlife "must go beyond the explicit teaching of the New Testament." Further,
he stated that "we are in the end on surer ground when as
Christians we claim the right to go beyond the letter, since we
do so under the irresistible leading of the moral principles of
the New Testament and of Christ himself." Here is great confidence to know the "spirit" in contrast to the "letter" (the
common-sense interpretation of the texts).

More recently it has become commonplace to argue that
universalism flows from the fact that God's true nature is that
of omnipotent love. The "hard sayings" of Jesus about hell are
not denied, but they are said to belong to what may be termed
"existential preaching"; thus they are never more than warnings, threatening people with the possibility that if they continue to refuse to repent (in this life and also in the next), they
will be damned. Omnipotent love, however, will finally win
over all people so that hell will not ultimately exist. The late
J. A. T. Robinson, for example, recognized that there were
what he called two eschatological "myths" in the New
Testament—that of universal restoration and that of final division into the damned and the saved.[17] The former is the
truth as it is for God and the latter is the truth as it is to us as
we are involved in a decision for the Gospel. God wills universal restoration and thus it shall be; nevertheless in preaching it is necessary to make people face the challenge. As God
is omnipotent love, what he wills he will bring into being by
eventually winning the loving response of all people. A similar position was advocated by Emil Brunner, although when
asked, "Is there such a thing as final loss or universal
restoration/salvation?" he said that there was no answer.[18]
This is because the Word of God that addresses us is a word of
challenge, not a word of teaching or objective truth.

This emphasis on the message in the New Testament about
judgment and Gehenna as essentially (indeed only) challenge, warning, and existential encounter has become fairly

common in recent theology and teaching; with it, of course, goes the further point that it is wrong to "objectify" this material into a *doctrine* of hell that can be made part of a theological system.

Universalism as the election of all people to salvation

Here we come to the view of the giant of twentieth-century theology, Karl Barth, set forth in his giant, Christocentric *Church Dogmatics*.[19] Since for Barth the whole relation between eternity and time is focused in Jesus Christ, it is also true that all human destinies are fulfilled in him in all eternity. Having refashioned the Reformed doctrine of predestination by making it wholly Christological, he could affirm that it is Jesus Christ who is both rejected and elected. God in Christ has taken upon himself the rejection which humankind deserves and also has in Christ elected all people to salvation. Thus the reconciliation of all to God has occurred, for Christ has died and risen. This means that the good news is the announcement that in Christ every human being is elected and has salvation. Logically this appears to mean that whether or not people believe or do not believe, all will be saved, for all are elected unto salvation in Christ. Though many accused him of being a universalist, Barth denied this charge and maintained that we may only hope that universal salvation remains a possibility. God, he argued, is truly free and since he has made threats in the proclamation that those who willfully disregard the gospel will be lost, we must allow that freedom to be exercised in the execution of damnation, if God so will: but Barth seems to doubt that he will.

Geoffrey Bromiley, the translator of the *Church Dogmatics*, thinks that Barth has a definite tendency to universalism and offers these words of criticism:

> What Barth fails to see is that to deny the possibility of salvation of all is no infringement of the divine sovereignty if God himself

has made it plain that all will not be saved. But on any reading this surely is the Bible's teaching. We may not know who will be saved, or how many, but we do know that there will be the lost as well as the saved. Hence the divine sovereignty cannot be invoked in favor of a state of suspense on this matter. Unless Barth is persuaded, and can show, that the biblical data are different, his hesitation here is a violation of his own Scripture principle.[20]

Whether or not Barth actually was an universalist is a technical question. His massive influence has been such that he has helped to make universalism a respectable doctrine to discuss and hold within the Church.[21]

Universalism in the Bible

Instead of listing arguments against universalism and offering a theology of the relationship of sincere adherents of the religions of the world to Jesus Christ, we shall indicate the "universalism" of the Bible:[22] namely, that there is one God and one way of salvation for all. "Salvation is found in no one else, for there is no other name (i.e., Jesus Christ of Nazareth) under heaven given to men by which we must be saved" (Acts 4:12).

Biblical universalism begins in the book of Genesis with God's great promise to Abraham that in him all the nations of the earth would be blessed. God has freely chosen to save the world through the family of Abraham and, as Paul indicates in Galatians 3 and Romans 4, particularly through Jesus the true seed of Abraham. This promise came from the God who required that his covenant people confess daily that he is one: "Hear, O Israel; the LORD our God, the LORD is one" (Deut. 6:4). Thus as there is one God who has made one promise (fulfilled in one Person, Jesus the true seed of Abraham) there can only be one way of salvation. To say that there are other ways is to deny the uniqueness of Jesus, the Christ, and is to suggest that there is more than one God. True universalism refers not to results but to marvelous possibilities for all people everywhere, irrespective of race, sex, or status. In Christ God has revealed the one way of salvation and in the gospel he calls all people to enter that way. Thus an integral part of the *missio dei* given to the universal Church is to preach the gospel to every creature so that all hear of what God in Christ has achieved for all humankind and thus all may repent and believe in the Lord Jesus Christ. The motivation for this evangelization of the world is rooted in God's love for humankind, revealed in the incarnation and specifically in the sacrificial death of the incarnate One at Calvary. 'God, our Savior,' Paul told Timothy, "wants all men to be saved and to come to a knowledge of the truth. For there is one God and one mediator between God and men, the man Christ Jesus, who gave himself as a ransom for all men" (1 Tim. 2:4-5). Further, this living God "is the Savior of all men and especially of those who believe" (1 Tim. 4:10).

The passages in the Pauline Letters which appear to point to a doctrine of universalism do, on careful study, refer either to the universal nature of the gospel (it is to be offered to all) or to the completion of God's purposes in Christ at the end. These passages are Romans 11:12,25-6; 2 Corinthians 5:19; Colossians 1:20; Romans 8:21; Ephesians 1:10; together with 1 Corinthians 15:25-8; Ephesians 1:20-23; Ephesians 4:8-10 and Philippians 2:9-11. Take for example the statement of Paul "that God may be all in all" (1 Cor. 15:28). In the context this refers to God's absolute sovereignty, when there will be no more opposition to him or to Jesus, the Mediator. All people, the godly and ungodly, and all angels, the good and the bad, will be compelled through the person and work of Christ to recognize God as the One and Only. The end will manifest the total and complete sovereignty of God; Paul cannot go higher than this in his thoughts. Thus biblical universalism allows not only for the universal offer of salvation but the universal judgment and the declaration there that God is truly all in all.

Notes

[1] *City of God*, xxi:17-27.

[2] There is a translation of *De Principiis (On First Principles)* by G. W. Butterworth (SPCK, London, 1936; Harper Torchbooks, 1966). For an exposition of *apokastasis* see J. W. Trigg, *Origen*, Atlanta, 1983, 103ff, and C. Bigg, *The Christian Platonists of Alexandria*, Oxford, 1913, 147ff. The latter also deals with universalism in Clement's teaching.

[3] Trigg, *Origen*, 249; Bigg, op.cit., 344. See also E. H. Plumptre, *The Spirits in Prison*, London, 1893, 138ff.

[4] See *The Seven Ecumenical Councils*, which is vol. xiv of *A Select Library of Nicene and Post-Nicene Fathers*, 2nd series, edited by P. Schaff and H. Wace, Grand Rapids, 1977, 316-17.

[5] For Erigena see the article on him in the *Oxford Dictionary of the Christian Church*, where there is a full bibliography. For Sterry and White see D. P. Walker, *The Decline of Hell*, chap. 7.

[6] Trigg, *Origen*, has much to say on this topic.

[7] Hebblethwaite, *The Christian Hope*, 216-17.

[8] See, e.g., the "intercessions" in the new *Prayer Book* of the Episcopal Church USA.

[9] Schleiermacher, *The Christian Faith* (ed. H. R. Mackintosh and J. S. Stewart, Edinburgh, 1928), paragraphs 117-20 and 163. See further Martin Redeker, *Schleiermacher: Life and Thought*, Philadelphia, 1973, 145ff.

[10] *The Christian Faith*, 550.

[11] Ibid., 720-21. Among those who taught such a doctrine are Tertullian, Cyprian, Augustine, Aquinas, Baxter, and Edwards. See further Walker, *Decline of Hell*, 29.

[12] Mackintosh, "Studies in Eschatology, VII, Universal Restoration," *The Expositor*, 8th series, 8 (1914), 130.

[13] J. H. Leckie, *The World to Come*, 276-77.

[14] Those who Leckie mentions are dealt with in greater detail by G. Rowell in his *Hell and the Victorians*, e.g., Andrew Jukes, *The Second Death and the Restoration of All Things* (1867); Samuel Cox, *Salvator Mundi* (1877); and F. W. Farrar, *Eternal Hope* (1878). For lists of seventeenth and eighteenth century books espousing universalism, see the bibliography by E. Abbott in W. R. Alger, *A Critical History of the Doctrine of a Future Life*, New York, 1878. And for literature on the American scene see the article and bibliography on "Universalism" by D. B. Eller in *Evangelical Dictionary of Theology* (ed. W. A. Elwell, Grand Rapids, 1984).

[15] There is a growing literature on the relationship of Christianity and other religions, but among the authors who seem to have encouraged the idea of universalism in this connection are John Hick, *Death and Eternal Life* (1976), Raymond Pannikar, *The Trinity and World Religions* (Madras, 1970), and George Khodr, "Christianity in the Pluralistic World: The Economy of the Holy Spirit," *Living Faiths and the Ecumenical Movement*, Geneva, 1971. Those who attend the assemblies and conferences of the World Council of Churches are very familiar with the tendency either to assert or to assume (as probable) universalism.

[16] It was published in *Immortality* (ed. B. H. Streeter, 1917), 167ff.

[17] Robinson, *In the End, God* (revised edition, London 1968). See the comments by S. H. Travis, *Christian Hope and the Future of Man*, 125ff. For a criticism of Robinson's first exposition of his views in the *Scottish Journal of Theology*, see his article "Universalism—is it heretical?" in vol. 2 (1949), 139-155 and the reply by T. F. Torrance, "Universalism or Election," in vol. 2 (1949), 310-18.

[18] Brunner, *Eternal Hope*, London, 1954, 183. See also his *Dogmatics*, vol. 3, chap. 10.

[19] See especially Barth, *Church Dogmatics*, Vol. 4, part 3, 461ff.; also Vol. 2. part 2, 470ff.

[20] Bromiley, "Karl Barth," *Creative Minds in Contemporary Theology*, ed. P. E. Hughes, Grand Rapids, 1969, 54.

[21] E.g., D. T. Niles, the influential Indian theologian, taught an incipient universalism that he appears to have learned from Barth; see his *Upon the Earth*, Madras, 1963, 90ff.

[22] In technical theology a distinction has often been made be-

tween absolute universalism and relative universalism. The latter describes the universal nature of Christ's death and the call of the gospel but does not deduce from these salvation for all people of all time.

Epilogue

We have now surveyed both the teaching of the New Testament and the Church in history on the subject of heaven and hell. Initially we accepted that heaven is not to be treated as the logical equivalent of hell, since by its very nature as God's unique abode and the sphere where Christ is exalted it can have no possible equivalent. Also we noticed that the preaching and teaching of Jesus concerning Gehenna, darkness, and damnation were in the context of his proclamation and exposition of the kingdom of God, salvation, and eternal life; they were never proposed as independent topics for reflection and study. This latter point has been much emphasized by distinguished theologians both in the Roman and Protestant churches.

With special reference to P. Althaus, H. U. von Balthasar (Roman Catholic), Karl Rahner (Roman Catholic) and K. Barth, the Dutch theologian G. C. Berkouwer has written: "The preaching of the last things, they argue, must be related to the sphere of faith and responsibility, and is not a matter of objective, theoretical, neutral postulates."[1] Thus they appear to favor universalism. However, this is not so, states Berkouwer, for their true position is that they reject *apokastastis* as a doctrine and maintain that "any conclusions outside the realm of preaching and responsibility are to be rejected, and all discussion of the judgment is to be related to the proclamation of reconciliation."

On preaching hell

Then Berkouwer suggests the proper way to preach hell. It is certainly to be preached but within the context of the full and universal proclamation of the gospel: Indeed it is part of the whole gospel and thus cannot be left out. If it is preached outside the proclamation of the kingdom of God, then as an independent topic it lacks genuine seriousness as a message from God. Berkouwer adds that it is not proper for disciples to want to know who exactly will be the members of the kingdom of God. He refers to the question put to Jesus, "Lord, are only a few people going to be saved?" and to the reply, "Strive to enter through the narrow door" (Luke 13:23-24). He makes the further point that judgment will begin at the house of God (1 Peter 4:17), that "many who are first will be last and the last first" (Matt. 19:30), and that not everyone who says "Lord, Lord" will enter into the kingdom. These comments are important and underline the fact that the gospel calls for obedience, trust, and love, not for discussion of the implications of parts of the message. Warnings, threats, and exhortations are given to be heeded, not to be treated as access to independent information.

The good news, we may suggest, is something like this: "Because God in Christ has provided salvation for you, you are to repent of your sins, believe the Gospel, and live faithfully as a disciple: To reject the Gospel is to place yourself in danger of hell, darkness, and damnation. God does not wish you to be lost but rather he longs that you will receive his offer of grace, pardon, salvation, and reconciliation."

So let us recognize and admit that to objectify hell and make it into an independent doctrine, a parallel truth, as it were, to that of heaven, is not encouraged by the way in which hell is presented in the New Testament. However, to say this does not mean that we are not to have any doctrine of hell: To warn people to avoid hell means that hell is a reality, or can be a reality. Thus it is unavoidable that we offer a tenta-

200

tive description of hell at least in terms of the *poena damni* (pain of loss of the beatific vision) and possibly of the *poena sensus* (pain of sense, i.e., via the senses) but refuse to go beyond the minimum detail and recognize always that we are speaking figuratively. Further, it is better in any systematic theology to treat hell when treating the gospel and not to leave it to the final section on "the last things," where it can so easily become a logical equivalent of heaven in the final order of reality.

A few more observations are in order. First of all, no person should take it upon himself to say to another person, "You are certainly going to hell." God alone passes such a judgment. Second, we cannot predict how many will go to hell: It may be many, a few, or none. God alone knows. Third, we must not deduce a doctrine of hell from a doctrine of predestination, in particular from a doctrine of double predestination. To do this is to make a logical deduction from an area which, while being a definite biblical theme (i.e., predestination), is also a theme that has the air of mystery in and around it and which is truly doxological by nature. Thus it is not suited to become the premise of a logical deduction. Fourth, discussion as to whether hell means everlasting punishment or annihilation after judgment may be interesting but is both a waste of time and an attempt to know what we cannot know. (Conditional immortality is basically a subject that does not belong to the discussion of hell but to the nature of human beings: Thus it is a legitimate topic for discussion, for it concerns what kind of creatures we are. As we noted above, while conditional immortality may lead to a doctrine of annihilation of the soul, annihilation as such does not require a doctrine of conditional immortality.) Fifth, great care is necessary in seeking to justify the need for hell in terms of divine justice and the punishment of sin: This enterprise raises all kinds of questions about retributive and remedial punishment and has to work from certain presuppositions as to the role and nature of God as Judge. And so we could go on. Sufficient has been said to make the point that belief in hell and description of hell call for great care not only by the preacher but also by the Christian disciple in day-to-day speech.

On heavenly-mindedness

Preaching and teaching and talking about heaven is altogether on a different plane, even though our language remains figurative and our attitude reverential. United to Christ as his body and filled with the Spirit as the temple of the Holy Spirit, the believing faithful belong to heaven, for there is Christ, and from there comes the Spirit. They are members of the kingdom of heaven and as such will be part of the new order of reality in the age to come. They must speak about heaven, for they belong to the heavenly Jerusalem, and the source of their faith, hope, and love is in, with, and through Christ in heaven. Though they experience heaven on earth through the ministry of the Spirit, this same Spirit makes them long to experience the fullness of the reality of heaven, both in heaven where Christ now is and in the life of the kingdom of God in the age to come. Thus the household of faith looks up and looks forward when it meets for worship, fellowship, and for the Lord's Supper (itself an anticipation of the banquet of the kingdom that shall be after the Parousia).

We live in days when the upward and forward looks often give way to the introspective and existential looks: Christianity often appears to be a this-worldly phenomenon only, where God makes life more joyful and comfortable to believers on earth, as they have little time to think of the heaven above or the heaven to come. It is here that we can learn from the past the art of meditation and contemplation upon heaven. This is an important element within both Roman Catholic and Protestant spirituality, but it appears to be neglected today. For example Calvin has a section upon *medita-*

tio coelestis vitae (which for him is the same as *meditatio futurae vitae*) in his *Institutes* and sees such meditation upon heaven and the future life as an indispensible part of Christian faith and worship.[2] And in *The Saints Everlasting Rest*, Richard Baxter gives much practical advice on how to begin and continue contemplation upon heaven. The point is that Christianity which is not oriented towards heaven is hardly worthy of the name. In terms of the values of the kingdom of God, those who are truly heavenly minded are the ones most likely to do the will of God on earth—a truth which is hardly recognized today within the emphasis upon relevance, social service, and immediacy. An ancient Collect expresses it in this way:[3]

> O God, the protector of all that trust in thee, without whom nothing is strong, nothing is holy; increase and multiply upon us thy mercy; that, thou being our ruler and guide, we may so pass through things temporal, that we finally lose not things eternal: grant this, O heavenly Father, for Jesus Christ's sake our Lord. Amen.

If the danger in the sixteenth century was to pass through things temporal as though they alone mattered, then how greater a danger it is today with a longer expectation of life in the context of affluence and the consumer society!

Because they belong both to heaven above and heaven to come, Christians are called not merely into a better life but a different one. And this life may be characterized in terms of its intensity, vastness, and permanence.[4] Let us reflect on each of these:

Intensity—"I have come that they may have life, and have it more abundantly" (John 10:10). True Christians are "not anemic or invertebrate specimens"; rather "they are men and women living with tremendous zest and concentration and, because of this, manifesting the most baffling and kaleidoscopic variety of character and activity, since God has taken over their individual personalities" and is developing them to the full. However, their lives are not merely activistic for activism's sake: The source of their strength and energy is in meditation and contemplation on God and his heaven.

Vastness—"If anyone loves me, he will obey my teaching. My Father will love him and we will come to him and make our home with him" (John 14:23). In choosing to follow Christ, the Christian has chosen to have God, and in having God he has everything in him. Therefore

> the Christian's horizon is not limited by the short span of seventy years or so that lie between the cradle and the grace, nor are the good things to which he can look forward confined to the prizes of wealth, comfort, power and fame which offer themselves to his ambition, or even to those higher goods of science, art and human friendship which one earthly life can contain.

He looks forward to treasure in heaven and to all that God will freely give him, knowing that he is a member of that vast number of angels and saints who now surround Jesus (Heb. 12:22-4) and who will constitute the membership of the vast new heavens and earth.

Permanence—"Father, I want those you have given me to be with me where I am, and to see my glory" (John 17:24).

> The most tragic strain in human existence lies in the fact that the pleasure which we find in the things of this life, however good that pleasure may be in itself, is always taken away from us. The things for which men strive hardly ever turn out to be as satisfying as they expected, and in the rare cases in which they do, sooner or later they are snatched away. . . . For the Christian, all those partial, broken and fleeting perfections which he glimpses in the world around him, which wither in his grasp and are snatches away from him even while they wither, are found again, perfect, complete and lasting in the absolute beauty of God with whom is no variableness, neither shadow of turning.

Christians who are aware that their life in and through Christ by the Holy Spirit has the characteristics of intensity, vastness, and permanence will also know how to live in this world. They will treat the world as the creation of God, as truly good because it is God's handiwork but yet not the highest good because it is not God himself. They will live in this world as those who know that it is God's but yet not their true home, for that is with Christ above; in this way this world itself will yield up to them joys and splendors, of whose existence and nature the "worldly-minded" are totally ignorant. They will experience the world's transience and fragility, its finitude and powerlessness to satisfy, not as signs that life is a bad joke with men and women as the helpless victims, rather as pale and splintered reflections of the splendor and beauty of the eternal God himself.

The meaning of "last"

We have recognized that because God is eternal and Christ is in heaven, communion and fellowship with God in Christ is possible now, through death and in the afterlife: We have also seen that the full glory of the world and age to come does not exist to be apprehended until God's purpose in creation and redemption has been fully achieved and completed. For what is eternal cannot be related to what is temporal in simple temporal terms.

Christians speak of the "last things," but there is ambiguity in the word "last."[5] When we think of the Parousia, general resurrection, and last or general judgment, we tend to think of them as the last events in time (the end of the line, as it were). Yet we recognize as we reflect that the idea of something which happens strictly last in time is self-contradictory. This is because we go on to think of a time when it will have happened, and therefore of something coming after it. And we speak of the new age of the kingdom of God with the new heavens and new earth, which follow the last judgment. This seems to take away from the word "final" or "last" as used of the Parousia, resurrection, and judgment.

However, the word "last," as the word "final," bears another meaning. Not only does it mean that which comes after everything else but also that which completes a process by bringing it to its purposed end. In this latter meaning the last event or final act is not merely one event among others, or the one that is the end of a line of events or acts, but it is an event of unique importance. Its importance is gained not primarily from its relationship to a previous series of events but from the purpose achieved when the series ends. This meaning may easily be illustrated. Take the last movement of the brush on a painting or the manipulation of the clay by the potter. This last event completes the work of art not merely in the temporal sequence but more importantly by bringing into being that which had been in the mind of the painter or potter from the beginning of production. The last event is also a beginning, the existence of a work of art. The last event initiates a fulfillment.

Thus when the word "last" is used in relation to purpose, it carries both the meaning of that which comes after all others and of that which fulfills the purpose of the whole. This fulfillment is the beginning of that achievement or perfection which is relative to the purpose of the series. The Christian believes, teaches, and confesses that the "last things" are last primarily because they fulfill the purpose of God, by bringing into existence that final state of the kingdom of God which the Creator and Redeemer originally intended.

It is significant that Jesus is not only called the Beginning, but also the End (Gk. *telos:* Rev. 2:16; 22:13) and not only the First, but also the Last (Gk. *eschatos:* Rev. 1:17; cf. 1 Cor. 15:45, "last Adam"). The End is also the Beginning, and the Last is also the First in the person and work of Jesus, who shall come from heaven to raise the dead, judge the peoples, and inaugurate the new order of the kingdom of God. God's purpose or objective is achieved in, through, and by Christ, as well as with Christ. Christ himself is the goal in the sense that he is God-with-us, and thus our God, and that he is also the Man, the Representative of the new humanity (i.e., the Representative who makes the new humanity present). Also Christ has the task given him by the Father of realizing this goal in us and in creation. His appearance from heaven will not only be the last event of the old order but also the first of the new order; further, by this appearance he will complete God's work in the old age in order to become the Center of the new age. In, through, by, and with him the End will be the Beginning and the Last will be the First.

Amen. Come, Lord Jesus.

Notes

[1] Berkouwer, *The Return of Christ*, 401.

[2] *Institutes*, Book 3, chapter 9. For a fine exposition of Calvin's approach to heavenly-mindedness see R. S. Wallace, *Calvin's Doctrine of the Christian Life*, Edinburgh, 1959, chap. 4.

[3] *The Book of Common Prayer* (1662): Collect for the Fourth Sunday after Trinity.

[4] I follow here my former teacher and now friend, E. L. Mascall, *Grace and Glory*, London, 1975, 74-82.

[5] I take these suggestions from O. C. Quick, *Doctrine of the Creed*, London, 1938, 246-47.

·APPENDIXES·

Appendix 1:
Encounter With Satan

It is too easy today, even for those who take the Scriptures seriously, to dismiss either deliberately or unconsciously the presentation of Satan, evil angels, and demons as the mythology (or uncritical presuppositions) of a prescientific age. Few people in the West today appear to possess either a consciousness of the supernatural/transcendent realm of heavenly servants/messengers called angels or of evil spirits called fallen angels or demons.

In contrast, Jesus and most of the people he encountered were conscious of another world, an unseen world from which came both good and evil spirits, either to serve the Lord or to oppose him. It is impossible to understand the New Testament unless it is recognized that angels, good and bad, were deeply involved in human affairs and human lives. The portrayal of Jesus in the Gospels reveals that though he recognised the reality of sin in human hearts and though he encountered opposition from religious leaders, he was also supremely conscious of being opposed by and fighting a battle against the army of evil spirits led by Satan. In fact this was the decisive battle of his ministry, for it was the transcendent background to his battle against human sin, false religion, and the curse of death. Thus it is not an exaggeration to claim that for Jesus himself, as well as for the writers of the New Testament, the future character of heaven and hell was determined by the nature and outcome of this conflict. If Jesus, the Christ, had not been victorious in this conflict, then he could not have opened the kingdom of heaven to all believers.

Identity of Satan

There is no speculation in the New Testament as to the origin of Satan, evil angels, and demons; their existence is taken for granted, just as it was in contemporary Judaism and in the books we call the Apocrypha and Pseudepigrapha. In the Old Testament Satan appears as an accuser or prosecuting attorney who impugns the integrity of Job (Job 1-2) or who challenges the fitness of Jeshua ben Jozadak to function as high priest (Zech. 3:1-2); his accusation is made to God. However, by the time of Jesus the belief in Satan as a malevolent accuser and originator of evil of many kinds had developed; the accuser before God had become the obstructor of God's plans and of human attempts to fulfill God's will. And in this role he was assisted by a company of evil spirits, themselves fallen angels like Satan himself.

Satan was known by a variety of names: the devil (*diabolos*), tempter (*peirazon*), evil one (*poneros*), accuser (*kategor*), enemy (*echthros*), plaintiff (*antidikos*), prince of demons (*archon ton daimonion*), prince of the power of the air (*archon tou kosmou toutou*), Belial, and Beelzebul. His army of assistants were called devils, demons, and evil spirits. Though Jesus taught that God had prepared hell for Satan and his assistants (Matt. 25:41), he knew that a necessary and unavoidable part of his ministry was to overturn the power of Satan so that God's righteous and saving rule could replace the evil rule and influence of Satan. God's decree of hell for Satan and evil angels depended upon the battle being won by his Messiah!

Jesus declares war on Satan's kingdom

There was no need for Jesus to proclaim his identity to Satan and his hosts, for they immediately recognized him as

God's Messiah and their deadly opponent. Mark records that "whenever the evil spirits saw him, they fell down before him and cried out, 'You are the Son of God'" (3:11). Further, Mark records a significant conversation between Jesus and the experts in the Law, called the scribes. These men from Jerusalem claimed that Jesus himself was possessed by Satan/ Beelzebul and that this explained why he could perform exorcisms so successfully. Such accusations revealed that these men were getting near to blaspheming against the Holy Spirit by attributing to Satan the work of God. But Jesus showed them how stupid was their position by giving a few simple illustrations/parables: "How can Satan drive out Satan? If a kingdom is divided against itself, that kingdom cannot stand. If a house is divided against itself, that house cannot stand. And if Satan opposes himself and is divided, he cannot stand; his end has come." Obviously the kingdom of Satan, though being invaded, was still intact and so Jesus added: "In fact, no one can enter a strong man's house and carry off his possessions unless he first ties up the strong man. Then he can rob his house." (3:23-5). He was giving notice that he would enter Satan's house to bind him and release the captives.

At a significant point in his ministry Jesus sent out the seventy-two disciples two by two to proclaim the advent of the kingdom of God. On their return they told Jesus that the demons submitted to them as they invoked the name of their Master. Responding, Jesus shared with them a vision which the Father had given to him: "I saw Satan fall like lightning from heaven" (Luke 10:18). This vision was prophetic, for the exorcisms of Jesus and his disciples were only tokens of victory; the real victory was to occur in Jerusalem in Holy Week. Perhaps underlying this picture of Satan is the Old Testament idea of him as accusing people before God so as to bring confusion and disorder into the working of God's will on earth. This sinister activity will end, for in seeking to accuse Jesus, the Christ, before God and in his efforts to thwart the progress of the kingdom of God on earth, Satan had over-reached himself and declared war on God and his Messiah. Thus he will fall, and so will his assistants, who are already submitting to the authoritative word and power of Jesus and his messengers. The latter, however, are not to rejoice that they have power over demons; rather they are to rejoice in the ultimate triumph of God's kingdom and that, since their names are written in heaven, they will share in that kingdom.

The gospel of John accepts Satan's great power in the world, for he is given the title of "the ruler of this world" (12:31; 14:30; 16:11), but that power is an evil power, for he is also designated as "the father of lies" and a "murderer" (8:44). Thus Satan is seen as influencing Judas to betray Jesus (13:27). Further, Jesus sees the "hour" of Calvary as the hour when "the ruler of this world" will be cast out (12:31), for his passion and death were to be a confrontation with Satan (14:30). In and through the suffering and death, Satan will be judged and condemned (16:11), and in the apostolic preaching this victory of Christ will be proclaimed. So Christ is portrayed as winning the decisive battle but not of concluding the war, which will carry on until his Parousia; however, in his name the disciples will be able to resist the temptations of Satan and deliver people from his hands into the hands of God.

Mark's gospel, having told in 1:13 of the initial conflict between Jesus and Satan in the wilderness and how the good angels came to minister to Jesus, describes three hours of unusual darkness as Jesus hung on the Cross (15:33). The power of Satan's darkness is revealed as the universe of light mourns the horror of the crucifixion. The earthly rulers who put Jesus on that cross are themselves the tools of Satan; it is their hour only because it is that of the power of darkness (Luke 22:53). Even Simon Peter was in great peril, and his own fall and subsequent restoration issue from the struggle between Satan and Jesus (Luke 22:31). Thus the words, "It is finished" (John 19:30), refer not to submission to death but conquest over the world of darkness. In expectation of this conquest, Jesus had earlier been able to tell the penitent thief that they would be together in Paradise (Luke 23:43).

God raised Jesus from death and then received him into glory, thereby vindicating him and demonstrating that he had won the decisive battle with Satan. So in the first recorded sermon from the apostles, Peter told the large crowd of Jews that "God has made this Jesus, whom you crucified, both Lord and Christ" (Acts 2:36). Salvation from sin, death, and Satan's power and salvation into the joy and righteousness of the heavenly kingdom was available in the name of Jesus Christ, the Lord. Thus the ancient canticle, "Te Deum Laudamus," has the verse: "You overcame the sting of death: and opened the kingdom of heaven to all believers."

Interpreting Satan

Biblical scholarship generally assumes that angels, good and bad, belong to the realm of mythology. However, it is also recognized that Jesus either wholly believed in the reality of angels, Satan, and demons or that he cleverly accommodated himself to prevailing views and talked and acted as if he did believe. It is the more likely that not only Jesus himself but also his apostles had no doubts whatsoever that God had created angels and that some of them, led by Satan, were in open hostility to his will and purposes. This means that Christians today have to decide whether Jesus was right or wrong.

Making this decision is not easy for western people, whose ways of thinking are deeply affected by the general view that this world/universe is all that there is and that within it there is or will be a rational explanation for most if not all things eventually. In western culture angels now belong to the realm of the fairy tale and appear on pretty Christmas cards and in children's nativity plays. Few people appear to think that they have any objective existence. However, there appears to be a minority of people who are prepared to believe that there are evil spirits who inhabit human minds/hearts, influencing them towards wickedness and depravity. And also there are those who believe that within the universe and especially within the structures of society there are evil principles at work: thus Satan is called "the personification of evil" by some who admit the existence of such evil principles but are not sure whether the principles are personal, invisible beings.

If we can shed the mental picture of angels gained from Christmas cards and that of Satan and demons gained from medieval painting, then we can seriously face the possibility that God created not only human beings on earth but also another type of beings for serving him in heaven. If the latter were created with a free will, then for some of them freely to decide to reject the sovereign will of God and go their own ways is relatively easy to accept. Further, if when God created angels (literally messengers) he made them with the capacity to move freely from heaven to earth and back again, then the involvement of angels, both obedient and rebellious, in human lives and affairs is not incredible. And it is also reasonable to think that when the kingdom of God is the more intensely being extended on earth, the rebellious angels will seek to oppose it and bring harm to those involved; thus the intense activity of Satan and demons in opposition to Jesus and the apostles. Regrettably, the spiritual receptivity of most westerners is at such a low level that they are incapable of either feeling the presence of good angels or of recognizing the presence of demons.

Appendix 2:
He Descended into Hell

In the *textus receptus* of the Apostles' Creed is the clause *descendit ad inferna*, which has been traditionally translated into English as "he descended into hell." A variant reading has *inferos*, which is used to translate "Hades" in the Vulgate of Matthew 16:18. *Inferna* originally meant the underworld, the realm of the dead and came to refer specifically to hell, as the place of punishment within Hades, in the period of the Middle Ages. However, the English word "hell" likewise had a wider meaning in the sixteenth and seventeenth centuries than it has now. In the AV (= KJV) of 1611 the Greek word, "hades," is translated by the word "hell" on ten out of the eleven occasions it is used. And as hell is also used to translate "Gehenna," the word hell has a wide meaning. In fact it originally signified "that which is covered over or concealed" and is etymologically related to *Höhle*, a cave.

Taking *inferna* to mean the place of punishment in the afterlife (cf. Dante's *Inferno*), medieval theologians portrayed Jesus, as a human spirit, descending into hell in order to triumph over Satan and his demons, and to announce to them the deliverance of the believers of the old covenant from their *limbum patrum*. We are all aware of the theme of the harrowing of hell in the art and drama of the Middle Ages. Calvin rejected the doctrine of the harrowing of hell and took this clause figuratively to refer to Christ's experience as our Substitute in bearing the curse and wrath of God against guilty sinners, especially revealed in his cry of dereliction on the Cross. In general this has been adopted by Reformed theology, and G. C. Berkouwer makes much use of it in his reflections upon the preaching of hell today.

The Lutheran position is stated in the *Formula of Concord:*

> It is enough to know that Christ went to hell, destroyed hell for all believers, and has redeemed them from the power of death, of the devil and of eternal damnation of the hellish jaws. How this took place is something that we should postpone until the other world, where there will be revealed to us not only this point, but many others as well, which our blind reason cannot comprehend in this life but which we simply accept.

In modern translations of the Apostles' Creed we have, "He descended to the dead." This is an attempt to convey the idea of *Hades* as the realm of the departed and remove the medieval doctrine of the descent into hell to triumph over Satan. This is a reasonable translation in that the origins of the doctrine of the descent of Jesus (in his death) into *Hades* are clearly there in the early Greek theologians, and it was from the Greek-speaking part of the early Church that the teaching was taken and made into an article of this western creed, where it was a late addition rather than an original article. Thus the original Latin of the Apostles' Creed translated *Hades* rather than *Gehenna;* only within the developing western theology did the idea of a descent into *Gehenna* become prominent, though it never totally removed the descent into *Hades*, the place of departed spirits.

Obviously by inserting this article, those who used the Apostles' Creed intended that it should add something to "he died and was buried." At least it pointed to his death being a real death with the separation of body and soul and the entrance of the soul into *Hades*. Thus while Calvin's explanation is thoroughly biblical, it can hardly be a right interpretation of this article. The meaning must be sought in the fact that in death, while his body remained in the sepulchre, Jesus in his naked human spirit passed through into that transcendent, supernatural realm of departed spirits. Whether he did visit as it were the gates of hell or whether he enjoyed the beatific vision without interruption we cannot wholly say. To be our Savior from death and its consequences he had to endure all that death means and do this really and truly. He died, was buried, and descended into Hades both as our Substitute and our Representative. In Resurrection his naked spirit/soul reunited with his body to be raised from *Hades* to the right hand of the Father in heaven.

One fruitful line of meditation upon the descent of Christ is to think of Holy Saturday as the day when Christ rested from his work of new creation. On the Cross he achieved victory of Satan and offered a perfect sacrifice for the sins of the world: His redeeming work was completed when he cried out, "It is finished!" He died, was buried, and in his naked human spirit descended into Hades. There on the Sabbath, which is the seventh day of the week, he rested, just as God had rested when he had completed the old creation. Having brought the new covenant and new creation into being, Christ, resting in the peace of Hades, saw what he had made: And behold it was very good. He looked upon the travail of his soul and he was satisfied (Isaiah 53).

Select Bibliography

Part One: Biblical

a. Reference Works

Apocryphal Old Testament, ed. H. F. D. Sparks, Oxford, 1984.
Apocrypha and Pseudepigraph of the Old Testament in English, ed.
R. H. Charles Oxford, 1913, 2 vols.
Greek-English Lexicon of the New Testament, by W. F. Arndt and F. W.
Gingrich, Chicago, 1957.
Interpreter's Dictionary of the New Testament, ed. G. A. Buttrick,
Nashville, 1962-1976, 4 vols. and Supplement.
New Bible Dictionary, ed. J. D. Douglas, Leicester, 1982.
New International Dictionary of New Testament Theology, ed. C.
Brown, Grand Rapids, 1975, 3 vols.

b. General Works

Baird, J. A., *The Justice of God in the Teaching of Jesus*, London, 1963.
Finger, T. N., *Christian Theology: An Eschatological Approach*, Vol. 1,
Nashville, 1985.
Gray, J., *The Biblical Doctrine of the Reign of God*, Edinburgh, 1979.
Guthrie, D., *New Testament Theology*, Leicester and Downers
Grove, 1981.
Harris M. J., *Raised Immortal*, Grand Rapids, 1984.
Hoekema A. A., *The Bible and the Future*, Grand Rapids, 1979.
Jeremias J., *New Testament Theology*, Vol. 1, London, 1972.

Kümmel W. G., *Promise and Fulfillment*, London, 1957.
Lincoln, A. T., *Paradise Now and Not Yet*, Cambridge, 1981.
Ridderbos H., *Paul: An Outline of his Theology*, Grand Rapids, 1975.
Rowland, C., *Christian Origins*, London, 1985.
Rowland, C., *The Open Heaven*, London, 1982.
Russell D. S., *The Method and Message of Jewish Apocalyptic*, London, 1964.
Ryder-Smith, C., *The Bible Doctrine of the Hereafter*, London, 1958.
Simon, U., *Heaven in the Christian Tradition*, London, 1958.
Smith, W. M., *The Biblical Doctrine of Heaven*, Chicago, 1968.
Strawson, W., *Jesus and the Future Life*, London, 1959.
Travis, S. H., *Christian Hope and the Future of Man*, Leicester, 1980.
Vos, G., *The Pauline Eschatology*, Grand Rapids, 1953.

Part 2: Historical/Theological

a. Reference Works

Creeds of Christendom, ed. P. Schaff, Grand Rapids, 1977, 3 vols.
Creeds of the Churches, ed. J. Leith, Richmond, 1973.
Enchiridion Symbolorum, ed. H. Denzinger & J. B. Umberg, Friburg, 1937.
New Catholic Encyclopedia, ed. W. J. MacDonald et al., New York, 1967, 14 vols.
Oxford Dictionary of the Christian Church, ed. F. L. Cross and E. A. Livingstone, Oxford, 1974.
Reformed Confessions of the Sixteenth Century, ed. A. Cochrane, Philadelphia, 1966.

b. General Works

Augustine, *The City of God*.
Baillie, J., *And the Life Everlasting*, Oxford, 1934.
Baxter, R., *The Saints' Everlasting Rest*, 1650, abridged edition, 1928.
Berkouwer, G. C., *The Return of Christ*, Grand Rapids, 1972.
Buis, H., *The Doctrine of Eternal Punishment*, Grand Rapids, 1957.

Calvin, J., *Institutes of the Christian Religion*, ed. J. T. MacNeill, Philadelphia, 1960, 2 vols.

Edwards, J., *Works*, Edinburgh, 1976, 2 vols.

Gerstner J., *Jonathan Edwards on Heaven and Hell*, Grand Rapids, 1980.

Hebblethwaite, B., *The Christian Hope*, Basingstoke, 1984.

Heppe, H., *Reformed Dogmatics*, Grand Rapids, 1978.

Hick, J., *Death and Eternal Life*, London, 1976.

Hodge, A. A., *Evangelical Theology*, Edinburgh, 1976.

Kelly, J. N. D., *Early Christian Doctrines*, London, 1968⁴.

_____ *Early Christian Creeds*, London, 1960².

Küng, H., *Eternal Life*, New York, 1984.

Leckie, J. H., *The World to Come and Final Destiny*, Edinburgh, 1918.

Le Goff, J., *The Birth of Purgatory*, Chicago, 1983.

Martin, J. P., *The Last Judgment in Protestant Theology from Orthodox to Ritschl*, Edinburgh, 1963.

Mascall, E. L., *From Grace to Glory*, London, 1975.

Pusey, E. B., *What is of Faith as to Everlasting Punishment?* London, 1880.

Rowell, G., *Hell and the Victorians*, Oxford, 1974.

Schleiermacher, F., *The Christian Faith*, Edinburgh, 1928.

Schmaus, M., *Dogma 6. Justification and the Last Things*, 1977.

Staudinger, J., *Life Hereafter*, Dublin, 1964.

Van der Walle, A., *From Darkness to the Dawn*, London, 1984.

Walker, D. P., *The Decline of Hell. Seventeen-Century Discussions of Eternal Torment*, London, 1964.

Winklhofer, A., *The Coming of His Kingdom: A Theology of the Last Things*, London, 1963.